Wise Up

10-Minute Family Devotions in Proverbs

"In *Wise Up*, Marty Machowski has given parents a thoughtful, creative, compelling, gospel-centered resource to train their kids in biblical wisdom and Christ-exalting living. Marty's love for his readers and the Savior are obvious throughout, and I was overjoyed that Sovereign Grace Music could partner with New Growth Press for this project. If you're a parent looking for help with family devotions, this is a gold mine."

—**Bob Kauflin,** Director of Sovereign Grace Music

"*Wise Up* by Marty Machowski is an excellent resource for family devotions. Over the course of twelve weeks, he provides engaging lessons that help families explore the wisdom of Proverbs in a five-day-a-week format. *Wise Up* uses songs, purposeful activities, and probing questions to draw families into the Bible, allowing them to grow closer to one another as they grow closer to God. Of all the activities we can do with our children, family devotions are the one opportunity we cannot afford to miss!"

—**Melissa Kruger,** Women's Ministry Coordinator at Uptown Church PCA; author of *The Envy of Eve: Finding Contentment in a Covetous World* and *Walking with God in the Season of Motherhood*

"In this volume, Marty Machowski has provided a precious gift to Christian families. In the pages of this book parents will find an accessible road map for sharing the riches of the wisdom of the book of Proverbs with their children. The author assists parents with this task by providing illustrative activities and songs, facilitating prayer, and by providing relevant questions aimed at unfolding the wisdom of God's Word."

—**Anthony T. Selvaggio,** Preacher; lecturer; author of *The Proverbs Driven Life*

"*Wise Up* will help your children see that a life of wisdom is honest, hard-working, forgiving, generous, and faithful. But best of all, Marty Machowski shows us that this God-fearing life will only be ours when our hearts are made new by Jesus, who is himself God's wisdom for us—our righteousness, holiness, and redemption."

—**Jared Kennedy,** Pastor of Families, Sojourn Community Church—Midtown Congregation, Louisville, KY

"Wise parents want to raise wise children. But life conspires to make us live less wisely than we'd like, or they need. *Wise Up* helps parents to live wisely and instill that wisdom in their children. By means of fun projects, daily Scriptures, insightful explanations, helpful discussion questions, and even memorable songs, *Wise Up* makes family devotions doable and enjoyable for everyone."

—**John Kitchen,** Senior Pastor, Stow Alliance Fellowship, Stow, Ohio; author of *Proverbs: A Mentor Commentary*

"I don't think I've met a parent who is satisfied with their experience of family devotions. And this is why I am grateful for Wise Up. Marty provides parents with twelve weeks of insightful and relevant family devotions from Proverbs. I heartily recommend this book to parents who want to create meaningful and memorable family devotions. Parents, wise up and buy this book!"

—**C. J. Mahaney,** Senior Pastor, Sovereign Grace Church of Louisville

"Marty Machowski has delivered yet another faithful, clear, and accessible book for parents and families. Wise Up is a compelling resource that winsomely communicates the wisdom of Proverbs to a modern generation, while also showing how Proverbs fits within the biblical storyline that culminates in the person and work of Jesus Christ. This book is a helpful tool for any parent who treasures the spiritual lives of their children and wants to nourish them in the faith once for all delivered to the saints."

—**R. Albert Mohler, Jr.,** President of the Southern Baptist Theological Seminary, Louisville, KY

"I am pleased to recommend another of Marty Machowski's wonderful family worship resources. Wise Up is a twelve-week study in the Proverbs. Each family devotional can be done in about ten minutes and includes Scripture reading, brief comments followed by provocative questions and a suggestion for prayer time. This book is engaging, interesting, full of good content, and above all doable—a valuable resource. Get it and use it for the good of your kids and generations yet unborn!"

—**Dr. Tedd Tripp,** Author, conference speaker

"Let's face it: it's relatively easy for us parents to go around spouting wisdom to our children, including wisdom from the Bible. The real trick is to learn wisdom without losing sight of the Savior who is wisdom. Wise Up does this, using the same brief format parents and kids have found so helpful in Marty's past books."

—**Jack Klumpenhower,** Author of *Show Them Jesus* and *The Gospel-Centered Parent*

Wise Up

Marty
Machowski

Wise

10-Minute
Family Devotions
in Proverbs

Up

New Growth Press, Greensboro, NC 27404
Copyright © 2016 by Marty Machowski

Cover Design: Faceout Books, faceoutstudio.com
Interior Design and Typesetting: Scot McDonald
Illustrations by Scot McDonald

ISBN 978-1-942572-74-9 (Print)
ISBN 978-1-942572-72-5 (eBook)

Library of Congress Cataloging-in-Publication Data

Names: Machowski, Martin, 1963- author.
Title: Wise up : ten-minute family devotions in Proverbs / Marty Machowski.
Description: Greensboro, NC : New Growth Press, 2016.
Identifiers: LCCN 2016007195 | ISBN 9781942572749 (print)
Subjects: LCSH: Bible. Proverbs—Devotional literature. | Families—Religious life.
Classification: LCC BS1465.54 .M333 2016 | DDC 242/.5—dc23
LC record available at https://lccn.loc.gov/2016007195

Printed in Canada

25 24 23 22 21 20 19 18   3 4 5 6 7

I dedicate this book to the many parents who desire to disciple their children and who do not give up in spite of the many temptations that seek to lure us away from this most important task.

Contents

This devotional is designed to help your family explore the wisdom of Proverbs together. Wisdom is a great thing to seek. Wise people know what to do and say at just the right time. Wise people know when to speak and when to be silent. They know how important it is to be honest and kind; they know how important it is to be a faithful friend. Most important, they know that wisdom starts with trusting God.

Many have studied Proverbs because they wanted to become wise like Solomon, but the path of wisdom is found when we realize that the wisest people in the world—Solomon included—only become wise when they turn to Jesus to save them from their sins. Proverbs can give us good directions for wise living, but it can't give us the power to follow those directions.

Jesus succeeds where we cannot. Though a King in heaven, he humbled himself to become a servant. Jesus completed the mission given to him by his Father by going all the way to death on the cross to take the punishment we deserve for our sin. Seeking after wisdom is a worthy goal, but it is only when we see that Wisdom is Jesus himself that we truly become wise. Studying Proverbs through the lens of the gospel indeed demonstrates that "something greater than Solomon is here" (Matthew 12:42).

Each week, *Wise Up* explores one of twelve themes from Proverbs to see which practical wisdom we can learn and how it connects to the good news of Jesus's life, death, resurrection, and coming return. Scripture reading, discussion questions, and "wisdom activities" make these studies memorable for everyone in your family.

To help you and your children remember and reflect on these truths, consider learning the songs from the Sovereign Grace Music album *Walking with the Wise* as you go through this devotional (http://www.sovereigngracemusic.org/Albums/Walking_with_ the_Wise).

Enjoy all of the practical direction in Proverbs, but remember, don't try this without turning to Jesus for forgiveness, help, and direction. Jesus lives in the hearts of his people, empowering them to become like him, the wisest King of all.

The Real Wise Man

The One We Must Learn to Trust

Day 1

Dig into the Word
Read Proverbs 1:1–7:

> *The proverbs of Solomon, son of David, king of Israel: To know wisdom and instruction, to understand words of insight, to receive instruction in wise dealing, in righteousness, justice, and equity; to give prudence to the simple, knowledge and discretion to the youth—Let the wise hear and increase in learning, and the one who understands obtain guidance, to understand a proverb and a saying, the words of the wise and their riddles. The fear of the LORD is the beginning of knowledge; fools despise wisdom and instruction.*

A proverb in the Bible is a wise saying. The Proverbs teach how to honor God in the way that we live. The sayings in Proverbs were compiled by King Solomon and other wise men. Some proverbs are easy to understand. For example, "let wise hear and increase in learning" (Proverbs 1:5), tells us to listen carefully to what teachers say so we can learn more. Other times proverbs are like riddles that are harder to figure out. For example, "If you really want to gain knowledge, you must begin by having respect for the Lord." When we read this we should ask questions: What does it mean to respect the Lord? How does respecting God connect to gaining knowledge?

The book of Proverbs is filled with lessons, advice, and insight into how to make wise choices. The phrase, "let wise people listen" (Proverbs 1:5) tells us to listen, but we have to figure out how to be careful listeners. Does it mean we need to look at the person talking? Or ask questions about what we don't understand? Or ask the speaker to repeat what was said? Or take notes?

The best part of all is that the book of Proverbs is God's Word. While Solomon and other wise people are the authors, the Holy Spirit worked in them, inspiring them to write so that in the end, God is speaking to us, and it is his wisdom we are learning. God will use the book of Proverbs to teach, correct, and train us in righteousness (2 Timothy 3:16).

Talk about It

▶ Who wrote the book of Proverbs? *(Solomon, among others)*

▶ How can God use Proverbs in our lives? *(God uses his Word to make us wise.)*

▶ What does it mean to have respect for God, and how do we learn to this? *(To respect God means to know that he is in charge of us—and the whole world—and to trust him with our whole lives. As we learn about God's holiness and our own sinfulness we will grow in respect for God . . . and, consequently, in wisdom.)*

Pray about It

Ask the Lord to help you listen carefully to what he has to teach you through your study of Proverbs. Pray through Psalm 34:11 together: "Come, O children, listen to me; I will teach you the fear of the Lord."

Get the Big Picture

Supplies: 100-piece puzzle (use one your children have not seen before); plastic bag large enough to accommodate puzzle pieces

Ahead of time, transfer the puzzle pieces to the bag and hide the puzzle box.

Show the children the bag with the puzzle pieces and ask them to guess the finished picture. They may be able to guess parts of the puzzle from key pieces, but not all of the details. Now show them the box with the puzzle's picture and have them describe it again.

Explain that you are about to begin studying a book of the Bible that has many little pieces called proverbs (wise sayings). Each proverb teaches a bit of wisdom and is a piece of a big picture. The big picture is learning how to love and trust God with our whole heart. God is good and only asks us to do what is good. When we look at God's awesome power and then out of respect obey what he tells us to do, we are living in the fear of the Lord.

After devotions put the puzzle together.

Day 2

Dig into the Word

Read Proverbs 3:5–6:

> *Trust in the LORD with all your heart, and do not lean on your own understanding. In all your ways acknowledge him, and he will make straight your paths.*

Life is full of choices. Some are good and some are bad. The trouble is that it is not always easy to tell the best choice. In Proverbs 3:5, Solomon gives us some good advice: Don't depend on yourself. Trust God and seek his will, and God will help you make a wise choice.

This doesn't mean life is easy if you trust God; sometimes God allows us to experience hard things to help us grow. And it doesn't mean we won't sometimes walk the wrong way and stumble and fall into sin. But it does mean we can trust God to be with us and to guide us every step of the way.

Think of a mountain climber connected to a rope and anchored to the rock as he climbs up a cliff. The rope is there with him the whole time to keep him from falling. At times the climber pulls himself up with the rope. When he does, he must completely trust the rope. That is the same way we are to trust God, not just a little bit, but completely, with our whole heart.

Proverbs does not tell us to trust in the Lord with all our *words*. It is easy to say, "I believe in God" or "I love Jesus," but not really mean it down deep inside. That is why we are told to trust the Lord with all our *heart*. Our heart is the deep place inside us that holds what we want, love, and believe. If we trust God with everything we want and love and believe, then we are trusting God with all of our heart. We'll learn more about the heart in next week's lesson.

**Sing together
"Where It All Begins."**

Chorus
Here is where it all begins
Here's the key to every door
It is when we know the fear of the Lord

Verse 1
When others try to draw you in
So you would join them in their sin
The fear of God will keep you safe
And give you strength to run away

Verse 2
The Lord will bless the ones who search
For wisdom in His holy Word
He'll keep them from the devil's snares
He'll give them joy and hear their prayers!

Bridge
To fear the Lord, is to stand in awe
To love what's right and hate what's wrong
To fear the Lord, is to grow in love
For our great God who rules us all

Song
of the
Week

WHERE
IT ALL
BEGINS

Talk about It

▶ Why didn't Solomon say we should trust ourselves? Why did he say to trust the Lord? *(Parents, help your children think through the many reasons why we should trust God and not ourselves. Help them compare God's attributes with our own: he is all-powerful, all-knowing, and all-wise, and we are none of those things.)*

▶ What does it mean to trust God with all our heart? *(Trusting God with our whole heart means we trust him completely. We don't just trust him when things are going well, or when we have to do something that's fun or easy. Trusting the Lord with our whole heart means trusting God all the time, in every circumstance.)*

▶ Parent, share a time from your life when you trusted God even though it was difficult. *(Think of a hard time where you were tempted to doubt, but saw God pull you through. Our children's faith is strengthened when we share our own experience of God's faithfulness.)*

Pray about It

Pray through Proverbs 3:5–6. Ask God to help you learn how to trust him with all your heart.

 Day 3

Dig into the Word

Read Proverbs 18:10:

> *The name of the* LORD *is a strong tower; the righteous man runs into it and is safe.*

This verse compares God to a strong tower that we can run to for safety or shelter. Imagine living in a city that comes under enemy attack. Once the battle advances and the enemy draws near, most people run and hide for fear they will be captured. Now imagine that you are one of those people. If you had a strong tower with thick walls and a heavy iron door, where would you go? You would run to the tower and bar the door behind you.

Solomon used the picture of a strong tower to teach us that when we are in trouble, we can run to God. We can do that by calling on him and asking him for help. Calling on God in times of trouble is like having a strong tower wherever we go. He is always faithful; he always keeps his promises. We live in him, and he lives in us. God will always help us in our time of trouble when we put our trust in him.

We can also run to God by going quickly to the Bible. The Bible is God's word to us. In the Bible God speaks to us. He reminds us of his love, his care, his mercy, and he tells us exactly what it means to trust him with our whole hearts. The people God gives us—our parents and teachers—can help us with their wisdom, but God is the real Wise Man! No one is wiser. God's perfect wisdom is recorded for us in the Bible. That is why we are studying the book of Proverbs. Solomon wasn't recording his own wisdom; he was writing down the wisdom he received from God.

Talk about It

▶ Why is a strong tower a good word picture for the name of the Lord? (*A strong tower can protect us from an enemy's attack. Its thick, stone walls and heavy iron door would keep us safe. God protects us from danger when we trust him.*)

▶ What are some things a strong tower could protect you from? (*A strong tower could protect you from wild animals, attacking armies, robbers, a windstorm, etc.*)

▶ What can God protect us from? (*God can protect us from evil and dangers of all kind—from things that might happen in this world, our own sin, and the devil. Through the death of Jesus on the cross, God delivers us from eternal death.*)

Pray about It

Ask God to show you that he is faithful in every circumstance, and that you can trust him as your strong tower every day in everything.

 Day 4

Dig into the Word

Read Psalm 28:6–9:

> *Blessed be the LORD! For he has heard the voice of my pleas for mercy. The LORD is my strength and my shield; in him my heart trusts, and I am helped; my heart exults, and with my song I give thanks to him. The LORD is the strength of his people; he is the saving refuge of his anointed. Oh, save your people and bless your heritage! Be their shepherd and carry them forever.*

Solomon grew up listening to the psalms that his father, David, wrote. David taught his son to trust God. He taught that God would guard and watch over those who place their trust in God.

God also gave special instructions through Moses for the kings of Israel, to help them follow God. (Read those instructions in Deuteronomy 17:15–20.) God said a king should not own too many horses, accumulate too much gold, or have many wives because these things could turn his heart away from God. Each year the king was to write down a copy of this law and read it every day to help him remember these important instructions. God knew that it was easy to forget.

Sadly, even though Solomon was known for his wisdom and was the author of many of these proverbs, he did not follow God's command. He collected thousands of horses and tons of gold and took many wives. He surrounded himself with so many things that he lost sight of God. In time he drifted from God and loved and trusted all his earthly possessions more than God.

Our great King Jesus didn't make those same mistakes (or any mistakes for that matter!). Jesus trusted the Lord with all his heart and obeyed the instructions for kings that God gave Moses. And unlike Solomon, Jesus followed his own teaching. For example, he told his followers: "Not everyone who says to me, 'Lord, Lord,' will enter the kingdom of heaven, but the one who does the will of my Father who is in heaven" (Matthew 7:21). Jesus always did the will of his Father in heaven. How amazing is that?

Jesus didn't just say he would follow God his Father and then live life for himself. He obeyed perfectly, even when it came to dying on the cross. As Jesus prepared for his imminent capture and crucifixion, he prayed to God, saying: "My Father, if it be possible, let this cup pass from me; nevertheless, not as I will, but as you will" (Matthew 26:39). Jesus never loved anything more than God. The "cup" Jesus mentioned in his prayer was the cup of God's wrath or punishment for my sins and yours. So when Jesus agreed to drink this cup, he was agreeing to take our sins on himself—which is what his Father asked him to do.

Talk about It

▶ Why did God tell the kings not to collect too many things, like horses and gold? (*God knows that the things of the world can turn our hearts away from God.*)

▶ What about us—can the things of the world distract us from God too? (*Yes, it is easy to love the things of the world more than God. We often trust and love things more than God.*)

▶ How can we know if we love something more than God? Give examples. (*Often when we are impatient or jealous or angry about something it's a sign we love something more than God. An example might be when you hit or yelled at someone who accidentally stepped on and broke your favorite toy.*)

Pray about It

Ask God to show you what you trust more than him. Ask God to help you trust him more than anything else.

 Day 5

Dig into the Word

Read John 11:20–27:

> *So when Martha heard that Jesus was coming, she went and met him . . . Martha said to Jesus, "Lord, if you had been here, my brother would not have died. But even now I know that whatever you ask from God, God will give you." Jesus said to her, "Your brother will rise again." Martha said to him, "I know he will rise again in the resurrection on the last day." Jesus said to her, "I am the resurrection and the life. Whoever believes in me, though he die, yet shall he live, and everyone who lives and believes in me shall never die. Do you believe this?" She said to him, "Yes, Lord; I believe that you are the Christ, the Son of God, who is coming into the world."*

Jesus came to earth to succeed where Solomon failed—living a perfect life and obeying God in everything. He also came to die, to take the punishment Solomon deserved for turning away from God. If we place our trust in Jesus and believe in him, we too will have our sins forgiven. So you see, in the Old Testament and New Testament the message is the same. We must place our trust in God.

In today's Scripture passage, we see how Martha trusted the Lord Jesus with all her heart. Her brother Lazarus had died and Jesus hadn't arrived in time to heal him. Even so, Martha knew Jesus was her strong tower. So when Jesus came into town, she ran to him.

Not long after, Jesus went to Lazarus's tomb and called him to come out, raising him from the dead.

Notice that Jesus wasn't just talking to Martha. The words of Jesus call out to us as well. He said, "Whoever believes in me." So you see, the promise of living in heaven forever is for us too, if we believe in Jesus and place our trust in him. In the end Jesus is our strong tower that we run to, to save us from our greatest enemies, sin and death. Now that Jesus has come, we read the book of Proverbs differently. When we read the words, "Trust in the LORD with all your heart," from Proverbs 3:5, we don't just think of God in general, we think of our Lord Jesus who God the Father sent to live a perfect life, then die on a cross to take our sins away.

Talk about It

▶ In today's passage what are the names Martha called Jesus? *(Martha called Jesus Lord, Christ, and the Son of God.)*

▶ What did Martha do and say that help us see she trusted in Jesus? *(As soon as Jesus came she ran to him. She said God would give Jesus whatever he asked, and that she believed that he was the Son of God.)*

▶ Do we need to trust the Lord? *(Yes we too need to trust the Lord. Parents, help your children see that they need to trust the Lord for everything. It is God who keeps their heart pumping, provides their ongoing health, food, and shelter. Most of all, we must trust the Lord, for the forgiveness we need because of our sin.)*

▶ Parents, recall a time when you experienced trusting the Lord in a deep way.

Pray about It

Ask the Lord to help you believe and trust him.

Week 2

The Heart of the Problem

All We Do Flows from Our Hearts

Day 1

Dig into the Word

Read Proverbs 4:23:

> *Keep your heart with all vigilance, for from it flow the springs of life.*

There are rivers of water below ground much like the rivers above the ground. Wells are dug to reach this underground supply and provide water for us to drink. Sometimes these underground rivers bubble up to the surface out of a crack in a rock. We call this a spring. If the spring water is clean, plants will grow abundantly around it and animals will come to the spring to drink. But if the earth below is contaminated with poisons like oil or radiation, the water could be deadly to drink.

Our speech is like a river flowing from our hearts below. Wrong words and actions spring from a heart that is not loving or obeying God. That is why it is important to pay attention to what is going on inside you. If you think sinful things, sooner or later they will come out as sinful speech or actions. Take for example a boy who wants with all his heart to go out and play. What happens when his mom tells him that he must finish his schoolwork before he can go out to play? What do you think might spring from his heart?

While it is important to keep watch over our hearts, none of us has the power to change a sinful heart of stone that doesn't love

God or want to follow his commands, into a soft heart that loves him. God is the only one who can change our heart. God sent his only Son Jesus to live a perfect life, and then die on the cross for our sin. When we place our trust in Jesus and ask him for forgiveness, the Spirit of God gives us a new heart, one that wants to obey and honor God. Once that happens, the words that spring up out of our hearts begin to change as we learn to live for God.

Guarding your heart means watching it carefully to see what lives deep inside. It is so much better to turn away from sinful thoughts or desires before they flow out as sinful speech or actions. When we do say something sinful or unkind, we can be sure that it flowed from a heart that is sinful and that the only cure for what is wrong with our heart is turning to Jesus for forgiveness and help.

Talk about It

▶ Recall a spring you have seen or look for a picture of a spring on the Internet to share with your children.

▶ What kind of sinful thoughts, feelings, or desires can we have in our hearts? *(Help your children see how words and actions reveal heart desires. Some examples: A child is envious over someone's new toy and considers stealing it for himself. You sneak more treats to eat after you were told that you've eaten enough. You sulk because the weather prevents you from playing outside. Notice that some of these things are good things—the problem is not that we want them [like playing outside], but that we want them more than we want to love and obey God).*

▶ Share a recent sinful thought or desire you had and what you did about it. *(Help your children see that God wants us to confess our sin and repent [turn away from our sin]. Help them see how selfish or mean reactions to people are evidence of sinful desires.)*

Getting to the Heart of the Problem

Supplies: two-liter plastic soda bottle with lid (empty and cleaned out), pin, table, water

Poke two holes in the bottom of the plastic bottle with the pin. Fill the bottle with water and observe the rate of water leaking out of the holes. Poke additional holes if your bottle is leaking too slowly. Set the bottle on the table. (You will want to use a table that won't be damaged by a spill. If you have a wooden table, place the bottle on a tray or cookie sheet.) Unscrew the cap and place it on top of the bottle askew, to show that it is not properly screwed on. After you have an obvious puddle, call your children over to the table.

Ask your children to look at the table and see if they can tell you what is wrong with the bottle. While they may immediately guess there's a hole in the bottle, make sure they notice that the cap is dislodged and that there is a spill on the table.

Now ask your children to get to the heart of the problem and figure out what's wrong with the bottle. Explain that often in life problems have layers. The obvious problem on your table is the spill of water. But there is a deeper problem to figure out. On the surface you have a spill to wipe up. But getting to the heart of the problem has you asking why questions: why is there water on the table?

Getting to the heart of the problem requires diagnosing the problem. In the case of the bottle, there are two obvious possibilities. First, the cap became dislodged after the bottle was shaken up (soda erupts when shaken and it could have bubbled out from the top); second, the bottle might be leaking.

Screw the lid on tight, then have your children inspect for a leak. While they are searching for the leak, explain that we are like the soda bottle. Often, when we don't get what we want, we pout or get angry. The pouting and anger is like the spill on the table—it is evidence of a problem. When we examine our hearts, we discover that the real problem is sin—we want what we don't have. It takes wisdom to get to the heart of the problem, whether it's a spill on the table or mean words spilling out of our mouth.

Pray about It

Ask God to help us keep a close watch over our hearts and to confess and repent of sinful desires that God helps us to see.

 Day 2

Dig into the Word

Read Proverbs 27:19:

> *As in water face reflects face, so the heart of man reflects the man.*

In other words, "when you look into water, you see a likeness of your face. When you look into your heart, you see what you are really like" (NIrV).

Have you ever seen a photograph of a landscape where mountains or trees are perfectly reflected in a lake? If you walk up to a pond on a calm day you can look down and see your own reflection in the water below. That is what the first part of today's proverb is talking about. People look in mirrors to check their appearance. Just like the water, the mirror reflects your image so you can remedy any problems: a tuft of hair sticking up out of place or a smudge of jelly on your face.

The second half of our proverb today tells us that our hearts reflect who we really are, just like a mirror. It is easy to blame others for the bad things we say and do, but the Bible tells us that our behavior on the outside is nobody else's fault; it's only a reflection of what is inside our heart. When God softens our heart and gives us the gift of faith to trust Jesus, not only do our hearts change, but what we say and do changes too.

Sing together
"Trust in the Lord."

Verse 1
My father said, "Don't forget my teaching
But hold on tight to my commands
For long life and peace they will add to you
Don't let love and kindness leave you
Write them down upon your heart
And God and people will smile on you"

Chorus
Trust in the Lord with all your heart
And do not lean on your own understanding
In all your ways acknowledge him
And he'll make straight all your paths
Trust in the Lord

Verse 2
My father said, "Don't be wise in your eyes
But fear the Lord and turn from sin
And God will heal you and give you strength
Look to Jesus to be your treasure
He's worth more than jewels and gold
For he's more precious than anything"

Bridge:
Jesus, you're my confidence, Jesus you're my hope
You will keep my feet from stumbling
Jesus, you're my confidence, Jesus you're my hope
You will keep my feet from stumbling

Chorus 2
I'll trust in the Lord with all my heart
And will not lean on my own understanding
In all my ways I'll acknowledge him
And he'll make straight all my paths
I'll trust in the Lord

Song of the Week

TRUST IN THE LORD

Talk about It

▶ What is a reflection? How does your reflected face compare to your real face? *(A mirror or pond reflects an exact, but backward, image. So if you have a dab of jelly on the left corner of your mouth, your reflection will have the dab of jelly on the right corner.)*

▶ How is our life a reflection of what is inside our heart? *(We want things, good things and bad. What we do tells us what we really want. So if we want something that belongs to someone else, we might reflect that sinful desire by becoming angry or even stealing what they have.)*

▶ Parents: Give an example of a time when you did or said something that reflected what was deep in your heart. *(This can be something sinful like when you said something angry, revealing anger in your heart. But it can also be something loving, like when a tear drops from your eye when you are sad deep inside. Try to help your child think of an example of the same kind of thing from their own life.)*

Pray about It

Ask God to help you see your heart for what it truly is. Ask him to give you the humility to ask others to tell you what they see.

 Day 3

Dig into the Word

Read Proverbs 21:2:

> Every way of a man is right in his own eyes, but the LORD weighs the heart.

Here's another way of saying the same thing, "A person might think their own ways are right. But the LORD knows what they are thinking" (NIrV).

God doesn't just look at our outward behavior; God watches our hearts too. God wants us to do the right thing, of course, but even more than this, he wants us to love him. God told the prophet Samuel that, "man looks on the outward appearance, but the LORD looks on the heart" (1 Samuel 16:7). In fact, it is easier to do the right thing on the outside than it is to change a wrong attitude in your heart. When it comes right down to it, only God can change our sinful hearts.

When David repented of sin, he cried out, "Create in me a clean heart, O God, and renew a right spirit within me" (Psalm 51:10). David also prayed, "Let the words of my mouth and the meditation of my heart be acceptable in your sight, O LORD" (Psalm 19:14). David knew he could not change his heart on his own; he needed God to give him a clean heart. Good for David—and good for us—this is a request God always answers with a glad yes!

Talk about It

▶ What did David ask God to do for him in Psalm 51:10? *(David asked God to give him a clean heart.)*

▶ Recall a time when God helped you not to sin. Maybe you didn't say that mean thing you thought of, or you forgave someone who had wronged you instead of holding a grudge.

▶ What do you think it means for God to make a heart clean? *(When God gives you a clean heart, he gives you the desire to want to love and obey God. Once we have a desire to love and obey God, good behavior comes from that good desire and our lives reflect that change. Of course that doesn't mean we are done with sin. That won't happen until we get to heaven, but we can learn to go to God and ask for forgiveness more quickly. Our Father in heaven will always forgive for Jesus's sake and the Spirit will help us to turn away from sin and love God and others.)*

Pray about It

Pray through Psalm 51:10: "Create in me a clean heart, O God, and renew a right spirit within me."

 Day 4

Dig into the Word

Read Deuteronomy 6:1–5:

> *These are the commands, decrees and laws the LORD your God directed me to teach you to observe . . . so that you, your children and their children after them may fear the LORD your God as long as you live . . . Hear, O Israel: The LORD our God, the LORD is one. Love the LORD your God with all your heart and with all your soul and with all your strength. (NIV)*

Before God led his people into the Promised Land (the land that was called Canaan then and is now part of modern-day Israel), he gave them the law, and he gave parents the important job of passing that law down to their children. God wanted the children of Israel and their grandchildren after them to love the Lord with all of their hearts. To make sure the children learned about God, Moses instructed parents to be a good example of loving God with their whole heart. God knows that children listen and watch their parents. Children will repeat what they hear their parents say, both good and bad. Children like to do what they see their parents doing. They learn to pray by watching their mom and dad pray. They learn to confess sin by hearing their parents confess. Children who see their father and mother loving God with all their heart have an example they can follow and will more carefully listen to what they say.

At first, King Solomon loved God, but his many things turned his heart away from the Lord. God used Solomon to write wise proverbs, but he was not always someone who loved the Lord with his whole heart.

But Jesus, who was so much greater than Solomon, always loved his Father with all his heart and obeyed God's law his whole life. When the devil tried to tempt Jesus away from loving the Lord with all his heart, Jesus resisted by quoting Scripture. One of the answers he gave was, "You shall worship the Lord your God and him only shall you serve" (Matthew 4:10).

Talk about It

▶ What is God most interested in: obeying him on the outside, or loving him with our whole heart on the inside? *(God is most interested in us loving him with our whole heart on the inside.)*

▶ How are your parents a good example for you?

▶ How do you know if you love something other than God too much? *(Think of things that you live for or that bring on anger when they are taken away.)*

Pray about It

Pray that God would help you to love him with all your heart.

 Day 5

Dig into the Word

Read Luke 6:43–45:

> *For there is no good tree which produces bad fruit, nor, on the other hand, a bad tree which produces good fruit. For each tree is known by its own fruit. For men do not gather figs from thorns, nor do they pick grapes from a briar bush. The good man out of the good treasure of his*

heart brings forth what is good; and the evil man out of the evil treasure brings forth what is evil; for his mouth speaks from that which fills his heart. (NASB)

Jesus talked a lot about the heart. Jesus knew that sin starts deep in our hearts where the things that we really want are hidden. It is easy to make excuses when we say or do something sinful, but the fact is, sin comes from our heart. Jesus said, "Evil thoughts come out of a person's heart …so do stealing, false witness, and telling lies about others. Those are the things that make you 'unclean.' But eating without washing your hands does not make you 'unclean.'"

Jesus said that it is not good enough to obey God on the outside; obedience has to start on the inside. Doing good works on the outside won't change a sinful heart on the inside. We need God to change our heart. That is why God sent Jesus to die on the cross. Jesus died to take the punishment we deserve for our sin. Then he sent his Holy Spirit to change the heart of anyone who trusts Jesus. Jesus said, "Whoever believes in me . . . 'Out of his heart will flow rivers of living water' " (John 7:38). Living water flowing out of a heart is a picture of how the Holy Spirit lives inside us and changes us.

The prophet Ezekiel wrote, "[The LORD said:] 'I will give you new hearts. I will give you a new spirit that is faithful to me. I will remove your stubborn hearts from you. I will give you hearts that obey me'" (Ezekiel 36:26 NIrV). While we can benefit from the wisdom of Proverbs by following the advice we find there, God is most interested in what is making us do what we do. God is most interested in what is going on deep in our heart.

Talk about It

▶ Who is the only person to ever live that loved God perfectly with all his heart? *(Jesus is the only person who loved God perfectly every day with his whole heart, for his entire life.)*

▶ Since we often sin because we don't love God with our whole heart, what are we to do? *(God tells us to confess our sins and turn from them, to ask for forgiveness, believing that Jesus died to take the punishment we deserve. When we do these things, God promises not only to forgive us, but to give us a heart that wants to love God more and more.)*

▶ Parents, over the course of your life as a Christian, how have you seen God change your heart?

Pray about It

Pray together that God would help you love him with your whole heart.

Week 3

Two Voices Call

Listening to the Voice of Wisdom

Day 1

Dig into the Word

Read Proverbs 8:1–11:

> *Listen as Wisdom calls out! . . . On the hilltop along the road, she takes her stand at the crossroads. By the gates at the entrance to the town, on the road leading in, she cries aloud, "I call to you, to all of you! I raise my voice to all people. You simple people, use good judgment. You foolish people, show some understanding. Listen to me! For I have important things to tell you. Everything I say is right, for I speak the truth and detest every kind of deception. My advice is wholesome. There is nothing devious or crooked in it. My words are plain to anyone with understanding, clear to those with knowledge. Choose my instruction rather than silver, and knowledge rather than pure gold. For wisdom is far more valuable than rubies. Nothing you desire can compare with it. (NLT)*

Solomon, who wrote most of the book of Proverbs, loved to create word pictures and stories to help those who read them remember important truths. One of the most famous word pictures is found in our Bible reading today where wisdom is described as a lady calling out to men leaving a city on a journey. The idea is that if they listen to Wisdom they will be blessed in life. Why is that true?

Proverbs goes on to tell us that Wisdom speaks what is right, true, and good. Imagine having a friend that you could go to for help, and he or she would always tell you the right thing to do, at the right time, and in the right way. That is what wisdom is like. Wisdom never steers you wrong.

Proverbs says that the voice of wisdom and following her words

Two Voices

Supplies: soda (10–20 ounces) in a plastic bottle, straight pin, six index cards or slips of paper

On the front of three index cards, write the words "Wisdom Calling." On the back of the same cards write the following directions (one per card):

"1. Ask permission to open the bottle of soda."

"2. Pour the soda into glasses and share it with everyone around you."

"3. Grip the bottle firmly when you unscrew the cap."

On the front of the other three index cards, write the words "Folly Calling." On the back of the same cards write the following directions (one per card):

"1. Shake up the soda bottle so it explodes when opened."

"2. Poke a hole in the bottle with a straight pin."

"3. Wait till your mom and dad are not around."

Procedure:

Place the soda bottle on the table. Lay out the "Wisdom Calling" cards on the right and the "Folly Calling" cards on the left. (The sides with the directions

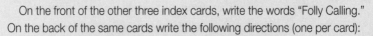

are more valuable than silver, gold, and precious jewels. Why would that be true? Think about it for a moment. Anything you can buy (a toy, a bike, or when you are older things like houses and cars) won't last forever. Toys break, you grow out of your bike, and even houses and cars don't last forever. But wisdom—following God and his ways—will last forever! That's why wisdom is worth more than gold and diamonds.

should be face down on the table. Only the words "Wisdom Calling" and "Folly Calling" should be showing.)

Explain that there are always two voices calling out to us. Wisdom calls with good advice and Folly with bad advice. Explain that the "Wisdom Calling" cards represent the voice of wisdom. Pick up the "Wisdom Calling" cards one by one and read them together. Talk about how Wisdom gives good advice.

Next, explain that even when we know the wise thing to do, the voice of Folly can tempt us to turn away from what is wise. Now pick up and read the folly cards. Discuss whether or not Folly gives good advice.

Ask your children if they felt any temptation to follow the advice of the "Folly Calling" cards. (Parents, if the children say they were not tempted, pull out the pin and excitedly ask them if they want to try shaking up the bottle, putting a pin in it, and seeing what would happen. They will most likely say yes. Then follow up their answer by asking, Do you feel the temptation to do something foolish now? Of course if they still don't want to that's a good and wise response!)

To satisfy your children's curiosity, take the bottle outside, shake it up, and carefully puncture the side with the pin. You can explain the science behind what is going on. The soda is mixed with carbon dioxide and placed under pressure. When the bottle is shaken up, the gas in the top of the bottle mixes through the soda. When you put a hole in the bottle the gas tries to escape out of the hole and pushes soda out in the process. Explain that you turned something foolish (puncturing a soda bottle inside for no reason) into something wise (a science experiment done outside where it is easy to clean up.)

Talk about It

▶ How does Proverbs describe the call of Wisdom? Why should we listen to her words? *(Wisdom's words are right, true, and good.)*

▶ Solomon and other writers wrote Proverbs, but who helped them to write down the right words? *(The Holy Spirit was with them as they wrote, so the words he wrote are really God's words to us.)*

▶ Look through Proverbs 8:1–11. Which verse do you think is your favorite or the most important to remember? *(Parents, let your children read through the verses and help them think through what is most important. There is no right answer. If your children are too young to read, read the verses again out loud and have them raise their hand after one they think is important or is their favorite. Pause for a moment after each verse. When you are done, ask your children why they chose the verse they did.)*

▶ "Wisdom is far more valuable than rubies" our passage today says. Try to explain this in your own words.

Pray about It

Ask God to change your heart so that you will love and trust God, not just try to do the right thing on your own.

 Day 2

Dig into the Word
Read Proverbs 9:13–18:

> *The woman Folly is loud; she is seductive and knows nothing. She sits at the door of her house; she takes a seat on the highest places of the town, calling to those who pass by, who are going straight on their way, "Whoever is simple, let him turn in here!" And to him who lacks sense she says, "Stolen water is sweet, and*

Sing together
"W-I-S-D-O-M."

Verse 1
There is something that's better
    than the latest toy
There is something that never
    can be destroyed
It's worth more than jewels and gold
Or anything money can buy

Chorus
W-I-S-D-O-M spells wisdom, I need it
W-I-S-D-O-M in Your Word, I find it
I need Your wisdom, Lord, each day

Verse 2
Left to my own self I always
    tend to go astray
But in the Bible You reveal
    Your perfect ways
You teach me to think like You
Instead of being a fool

Bridge
· I wanna love it, live it, learn it,
    read it (W-I-S-D-O-M!)
I wanna know it, think it, speak it,
    breathe it (W-I-S-D-O-M!)
I wanna love it, live it, learn it,
    read it (W-I-S-D-O-M!)
I wanna know it, think it, speak it,
    breathe it, yeah!

bread eaten in secret is pleasant." But he does not know
that the dead are there, that her guests are in the depths
of [the grave].

There's a woman named Wisdom who wants to show you all the good things. But there's another woman, named Folly, who doesn't want you to listen to Wisdom. You know how she does it? She yells really, really loud—she is so loud that it makes it hard to hear any other voices. She especially doesn't want you to hear the voice of Wisdom. She's not only loud; she's tricky. She's tricky on purpose; she's trying to trip you up. She wants bad things for you. She tries to get you to trust her and come into her house. But her house is not a safe house. It is a place where she wants to keep you locked up. She does not care about you; she is a liar. She wants to see you unhappy and ruined.

Imagine your mom is baking cookies for another family. You know they are not for you, but you take one anyway. Then the voice of Folly in your head says: "Uh-oh, you'd better run to your room and eat it in secret so you don't get caught."

When you choose to do wrong, when you choose to hide what you've done and lie about it, you're choosing to make Folly—this tricky, mean lady—your best friend. You and Folly are buddies in crime. There's only one path: you can go toward Jesus or away from Jesus. If Folly is your best friend, you are doing exactly as she planned; you are walking away from Jesus.

When Proverbs talks about having two choices it might sound like we have a fifty-fifty chance of getting it right. The truth is, however, that none of us would choose wisdom on our own. None of us would choose to trust and love God. We would only choose to rebel against God and do our own thing. Choosing God is righteousness; choosing self is sin. The Bible puts it this way:

No one is right with God, no one at all. No one understands.

No one trusts in God. All of them have turned away. They have all become worthless. No one does anything good, no one at all. (Romans 3:10–12 NLT)

So you see it's pretty clear why we need Jesus. Jesus lived a perfect life and then died on the cross to take our punishment for sin. When we accept Jesus as the sacrifice for our sin, God gives us a new heart—a heart that can obey him.

Talk about It

▶ Folly and Wisdom have already been talking to you. Share a time when you chose to be friends with Folly. Share a time you listened to Wisdom.

▶ What comes from listening to the voice of Folly? How can you listen to the voice of Wisdom instead? *(Listening to Folly brings bad consequences. The worst consequence is that obeying Folly's voice means you are walking away from Jesus.)*

▶ What is our only hope for choosing God's path of wisdom? *(Our only hope is to first trust in Jesus to give us a new heart.)*

▶ "All of them have turned away. They have all become worthless. No one does anything good, no one at all" (Romans 3:12 NLT). Does this mean there's no hope for us? *(There is hope for us. When we tell Jesus we are sorry for listening to the voice of Folly, he forgives us every time. See 1 John 1:9–10.)*

Pray about It

Ask God to help you recognize and say no to Folly and stay on the path of wisdom.

Day 3

Dig into the Word
Read Proverbs 1:20–27:

> *Wisdom shouts in the streets. She cries out in the public square. She calls to the crowds along the main street, to those gathered in front of the city gate: "How long, you simpletons, will you insist on being simpleminded? How long will you mockers relish your mocking? How long will you fools hate knowledge? Come and listen to my counsel. I'll share my heart with you and make you wise. I called you so often, but you wouldn't come. I reached out to you, but you paid no attention. You ignored my advice and rejected the correction I offered. So I will laugh when you are in trouble! I will mock you when disaster overtakes you—when calamity overtakes you like a storm, when disaster engulfs you like a cyclone, and anguish and distress overwhelm you." (NLT)*

Folly is loud, very loud; but Wisdom is loud too. Wisdom wants what is best for you. Wisdom wants you to walk on the good path toward Jesus. We can be sinful and choose Folly's way. Wisdom wants us to know that listening to Folly is dangerous and makes no sense. Wisdom wants us to come to her to learn and be wise. We can hear Wisdom's voice every day, but we often ignore it. We go after the shiny things offered by Folly, not seeing clearly that Folly wants to trick us into being her servants.

We won't always hear Wisdom's voice, but we hear it today. And today is the day we must listen to it. Remember this: Wisdom's voice is Jesus's voice. If you love Jesus, you will listen to Wisdom. If you have made Folly your best friend, you will ignore the voice of Wisdom. Will you listen to Wisdom today? Will you listen to Jesus today?

Talk about It

▶ What is a consequence? Give an example of a good consequence and a bad consequence.

▶ What kind of consequences will we get if we follow the call of Wisdom?

▶ What kind of consequences will we get if we listen to Folly?

▶ See if you can come up with bad consequences that result from listening to the following calls of Folly:

> Don't get up for school, you can keep on sleeping. (*You could miss your ride or miss class. If you do that too many times, your grades will suffer, you might need to stay after school as punishment, or you could even have to repeat a grade.*)

> Don't do your homework because you can probably just copy someone else's. (*Not only will you not learn anything from copying someone else's work, you will also get caught for cheating—which has a lot of bad consequences attached to it!*)

> Go ahead and steal from the store if you really want something. (*Folly wants you to believe you won't get caught, but people get caught stealing every day and they are arrested and sent to jail.*)

> You can get along fine without God. (*Trying to live life without God is risky business. You will have no real, lasting love or joy or peace, and you will have no one to stand beside you when you come before God after you die. There is only one way to get to heaven and that is by trusting and believing in Jesus.*)

Pray about It

Ask God to help you listen carefully to Wisdom by trusting him and by reading his Word.

Day 4

Dig into the Word

Read 1 Corinthians 1:24–25, 30:

> *But to those who are called, both Jews and Greeks, Christ [is] the power of God and the wisdom of God. For the foolishness of God is wiser than men, and the weakness of God is stronger than men. . . And because of him you are in Christ Jesus, who became to us wisdom from God, righteousness and sanctification and redemption.*

That last bit might be a little hard to understand, but it just means that Jesus "makes us right with God. He makes us holy and sets us free" (NIrV).

In today's Bible passage, Christ is called "God's power and God's wisdom." Jesus is Wisdom. Jesus came down from heaven to bring us the greatest words of wisdom of all time—the words of life. Here are some of the things Jesus said:

"Whoever hears my word and believes him who sent me has eternal life. He does not come into judgment, but has passed from death to life." (John 5:24)

"Let not your hearts be troubled. Believe in God; believe also in me." (John 14:1)

"Whoever does not love me does not keep my words. And the word that you hear is not mine but the Father's who sent me." (John 14:24)

The words of wisdom in Proverbs point to a day when God would send his Son Jesus as the living Word and living Wisdom. Jesus would speak the life-giving Word of his Father to tell us how to become children of God. The apostle John tells us that Jesus lived as the "Word" in heaven and then came down to earth as a man to live with us (John 1:1, 14). There is no greater wisdom than to obey God's Word since God's Word is always perfect.

We all need to listen for the voice of Jesus in God's Word calling to us to come and believe that he died on the cross and rose from the dead so that we can live with the Father in heaven. Jesus is the perfect voice of wisdom calling. Will you follow his voice?

Talk about It

▶ How well did Jesus follow the voice of Wisdom? *(Jesus never turned away from God's wisdom.)*

▶ What does it mean to follow Jesus's voice? *(We have Jesus's words recorded in the Bible. Jesus spoke to his disciples, but when we read his words they also speak to us.)*

▶ How can you know that you are following Jesus's voice?

Pray about It

Ask God to help you know and believe Jesus as true Wisdom.

 Day 5

Dig into the Word

Read Proverbs 2:6–8:

> *For the LORD gives wisdom; from his mouth come knowledge and understanding; he stores up sound wisdom for the upright; he is a shield to those who walk in integrity, guarding the paths of justice and watching over the way of his saints.*

The most important voice of all is God's voice. Solomon wanted his children to know and remember that God speaks knowledge and understanding. That means he always tells us the truth and we can learn how to walk through life's challenges from the truth he gives us. At first we might wonder, *How can we hear the voice of someone we can't see?* Well, God has given us his voice written down. That is why we call the Bible the Word of God. The Book of Proverbs is one small part of God's Word, which is why we are studying it.

God wrote the Bible using many different people who were inspired by the Holy Spirit. While the words they used were their own, God gave them the insight and truth to write. Those who wrote Proverbs knew that what they wrote were God's words. That is why Proverbs 2:6 says wisdom, knowledge, and understanding come from God's "mouth." God's voice is the ultimate voice of wisdom, and if we follow what he tells us to do in his Word, we will be wise.

God is perfectly righteous (that means everything God does is right), and he always does good. That is why we can trust God's Word and follow it. The voice of God will always lead us down the right path.

Psalm 119:105 says that God's Word is "a lamp to my feet and a light to my path." God uses his Word to light up our path and help us make wise, good, true, and right choices. God's Word teaches us the difference between good and evil and the difference between truths and lies.

Talk about It

▶ Whose voice is the most important voice of all to listen to? *(God's voice is the most important voice for us to listen to.)*

▶ How can we hear God's voice? *(God wrote down all that he wanted to tell us. That is why we call the Bible God's Word. The Bible is God's voice to his people, written down for us to read.)*

▶ Why can we trust God's Word? *(God's Word is true and always leads us down the right path.)*

▶ Why does Psalm 119:105 compare God's Word to a lamp to

light up our path? *(We cannot see the correct path in darkness. Just as a lamp lights a path at night, so God's Word helps us see the right choices to make in life.)*

Pray about It

Ask God to increase your desire to hear his voice and study his Word.

Two Paths

Recognizing the Path of Righteousness

Day 1

Dig into the Word

Read Proverbs 4:14–17:

> *Do not enter the path of the wicked, and do not walk in the way of the evil. Avoid it; do not go on it; turn away from it and pass on. For they cannot sleep unless they have done wrong; they are robbed of sleep unless they have made someone stumble. For they eat the bread of wickedness and drink the wine of violence.*

Last week we talked about the two voices that are calling us: the voice of wisdom and the voice of folly. This week we are going to look at a similar word picture, that of two paths. Folly tries to lure us down the path of wickedness and evil, while wisdom calls us to follow the path of righteousness. Again and again Proverbs shows us that we have choices to make—we can trust and follow God and his voice of wisdom, or we can trust and follow our own desires.

If you have ever taken a hike through the woods, you know there are good paths and bad paths. Good paths take you where you want to go safely. Bad paths lead you into dangerous situations—to the gravelly edge of a cliff or into a smelly swamp, for example.

Life can be pictured as a walk along a path. Sinful choices that we make are pictured as leaving the right path and entering the path of the wicked. Imagine walking along a path through the woods when two other children invite you to take a side path, one that you know leads to a large underground hornet's nest. If you go down that path, you know you could get stung.

Sin and temptation work like that. Others can tempt us to go down the wrong path. They want us to do what we are not supposed to do. They want us to stumble. Proverbs offers clear counsel: "Do not enter the path of the wicked." Solomon taught that the wrong path leads to death (Proverbs 14:12), but the right path leads to life (Matthew 7:14).

Talk about It

▶ Have you ever gone on a hike and seen a path or trail that was dangerous? *(Help your children remember a dangerous path they took on a hike, or perhaps if you live in the city you could talk about a narrow street with busy traffic that is dangerous to walk along.)*

▶ Describe what the picture in Proverbs of walking on a path is really about. *(It's about choices we make in everyday life.)*

▶ What should you do if tempted to walk down an evil path? *(Here are a few principles: keep eyes straight ahead, pick up your pace, don't stop to listen to temptation, most importantly, call out to Jesus for help.)*

Pray about It

Ask God to help you avoid the path of evil.

Right Way, Wrong Way

Supplies: large metal serving spoon, drinking glass

Gather around the kitchen faucet. Explain to your children that there are two paths to follow in life. First, there is the right way that follows God's Word and leads to good consequences, and second, the wrong way that rejects God's Word and leads to bad consequences.

Following God's Word is like driving a car on a highway in heavy traffic. If you follow the rules of the road and drive safely, you can travel many miles and never have an accident. Rejecting God's Word is like driving the wrong way on a highway during rush hour. Even a good driver has little hope of avoiding a crash. Some people think they can disobey God's Word and still escape bad consequences. But just like driving against traffic in rush hour will result in a crash, disobeying God's Word will also result in bad consequences.

Turn on the faucet, full force, and demonstrate with the spoon. Explain that the water flowing out of the faucet is the highway and your spoon a car. Run the spoon quickly with the flow of the water down to demonstrate there is no splashing—no "crashing of your car." Now do the opposite. With the spoon "cupped side" facing the ceiling quickly run the spoon upward from the bottom of the sink through the flow of water toward the ceiling to create the greatest splash (crash) you can create. Use this to demonstrate the consequences of going the wrong way.

Then demonstrate the right way and wrong way to try to fill the glass. You can hold the glass under the stream of water upside-down and sideways and you will get no water inside. But if you follow the right path and hold the glass upright, it fills to the brim with water. We have daily choices in life—to do things the right way or the wrong way. This week's Bible theme is taking the right path.

Day 2

Dig into the Word

Read Proverbs 4:18–19:

> But the path of the righteous is like the light of dawn, which shines brighter and brighter until full day. The way of the wicked is like deep darkness; they do not know over what they stumble.

Imagine being lost in a dark forest where overgrown paths can lead into danger with no escape. Then, just when you think there is no hope of ever finding the right path, you notice a new path—one that you passed by earlier. Then imagine how happy and relieved you would be to catch a glimpse of light ahead and realize this new path is leading you out of the forest. With each step, the forest thins and the sun shines brighter, until at last you are out in a wide-open, sunlit field! This is how Proverbs pictures the blessings of walking the righteous path.

The word *righteous* refers to what is right and good. The righteous person loves God and wants to please him. The righteous person walks toward the light, letting God's righteous light expose sin in his heart. The evil person, on the other hand, wanders in the darkness, stumbling over unseen obstacles, eager to hide his sin.

When it comes to choosing the right path, we need to ask ourselves why we are making the choice we are. You can choose the right path for the wrong reasons. Some people choose to follow the right path to make themselves look good or try to earn God's love. It makes sense to avoid danger, but we should also choose the right path out of love for God and because we want to please him.

None of us will always choose the right path on our own. That is

Sing together
"Make Me Wise."

Verse 1
Solomon was a young man
When he learned that he'd be king
He feared the Lord like his father
So God said, "Ask for anything"

Verse 2
He didn't ask for superpowers *(no, he didn't)*
Or to be a millionaire
He only asked God for one thing *(yes, he did)*
And gladly God heard his prayer

Chorus
Make me wise, make me wise
Let me see through this world's lies
There are so many paths to follow
And I don't want to compromise
Make me wise, make me wise
So I'm pleasing in Your sight
Lord, I want to bring You glory
So I'm asking You to make me wise

Verse 3
God is ready to help us *(yes, He is)*
When we call upon His name
He gives His grace to the humble *(yes, He does)*
Who, just like Solomon, pray

why Jesus died for us. Once we trust Jesus and realize that all of our sins are forgiven, his Spirit lives in us and we begin to follow him.

So why are you trying to walk the right path? Are you trying to be good all by yourself? Are you trying to look good so people will admire you? Or, are you walking the right path to please God?

Talk about It

▶ Have you ever been in a forest so thick that it was dark on a sunny day? How would it feel to find your way out to bright sunshine again?

▶ What does the word *righteous* mean? *(Righteous is about rightness and God-likeness.)*

▶ What does it look like for you to walk the righteous path? *(Parents help your children think about both outward behavior and what they think and feel in their heart. It is important that we not only do the right thing, but also that we think and feel the right things.)*

Pray about It

Ask God to help you every day to walk on the righteous path and to turn away from the path of darkness and sin.

 Day 3

Dig into the Word

Read Proverbs 22:5–6:

> *Thorns and snares are in the way of the crooked [or evil]; whoever guards his soul will keep far from them. Train up a child in the way he should go; even when he is old he will not depart from it.*

Did you ever notice that you never have to teach little children how to demand their own way? Because we are born with sinful hearts, nobody ever had to teach us how to tell a lie, or how to get angry when we don't get what we want. It's not the same with doing what is right: that has to be taught.

In today's Scripture passage, we see how important it is to teach a child what is right ("the way he should go"). What we learn as children can stay with us all our lives. Think about tying your shoe. You learn how to tie a shoe when you are only four or five years old, but it stays with you for the rest of your life. Or what about riding a bike? Once you know how to ride, they say you never forget. Even if you've not ridden a bike for twenty years, you can jump on a bike and you don't have to learn how to balance again.

It is important for children to learn that there are only two paths: the right path and the evil path; the way of wisdom and the way of folly. In the world today, it sounds like we can choose among many paths. This is wrong. The earlier we learn that we only have two choices, the better it is. We can walk toward God and light and righteousness, or we can walk away from God, toward evil and darkness. Once you can recognize the right way from the wrong way—God's way from the evil way—it will serve you all your life.

Talk about It

▶ What did you learn when you were young that you never forgot? *(Parents, help your children think through the things they've learned. You can start with tying their shoes and riding a bike.)*

▶ What can we do to stay on the right path? *(Again, draw your children out regarding what they've learned about recognizing evil.)*

▶ Can you remember a time when you were faced with a choice about whether to walk on the right path? *(Parents, share something from your own experience.)*

Pray about It

Thank the Lord for giving you parents to teach you about God and his ways while you are young. Ask God to help you remember all your life what they've taught you.

 Day 4

Dig into the Word

Read Proverbs 16:25:

> *There is a way that seems right to a man, but its end is the way to death.*

Wise hikers travel with a compass or GPS to guide them. They know that one patch of woods can look a lot like another patch of woods. It is easy to get turned around and lose your way. They depend on their compass or GPS to guide them because they know their mind can play tricks in the deep forest. Imagine getting lost where the road that leads the way out is only a hundred feet to your right, but you are sure in your mind that left is the correct direction to go. You could hike for hours trying to find the road, making your problems worse with each step.

Did you know that Jesus called himself the "Way"? Jesus said, "I am the way, the truth, and the life. No one can come to the Father except through me" (John 14:6). The most important choice any of us will ever make is between following Jesus—the Way—and following anything or anybody else. Proverbs warns us that we can't depend on what we think is right, because in the end, if we are wrong, it can lead to death.

So if what we think is not dependable, then what is? God's Word of course! God's Word is like a compass or GPS for life. It helps us stay on the right path without wandering off one way or the other.

For example, Solomon followed God's Word for many years. But late in life, he turned away from God and started worshiping idols. Imagine, the king known for his wisdom being so foolish as to abandon the Lord who had given him everything.

Talk about It

▶ Hikers use a compass or GPS to help find their way and stay on the right path. What does God give us to help us stay on the right path? *(God gives us his Word, which tells us the right way to go.)*

▶ What could happen to us if we reject God's Word and go the way that seems right to us? *(It could lead to death.)*

▶ Can you think of a Bible verse that helps you stay on the right path? *(Parents help your children connect the Bible to their lives. Here are a few good verses: "Children obey your parents in the Lord, for this is right" [Ephesians 6:1]. "You shall love the LORD your God with all your heart and with all your soul and with all your might" [Deuteronomy 6:5].)*

Pray about It

Ask God to help you always remember his Word and use it as your compass in life.

 Day 5

Dig into the Word

Read Luke 9:51–53:

> *When the days were approaching for His ascension, He was determined to go to Jerusalem; and He sent messengers on ahead of Him, and they went and entered a village of the Samaritans to make arrangements for*

*Him. But they did not receive Him, because He was
traveling toward Jerusalem. (NASB)*

Jesus followed God's Word all his days. This kept him on the right
path, even though he knew that would lead to him dying on a cross
for our sin.

When Satan came to tempt him off the path, Jesus quoted God's
Word. Jesus followed the plan God set out for him. Jesus walked the
path of righteousness and he walked it in constant closeness with
his Father through prayer. Jesus said, "The Son can do nothing by
himself. He can do only what he sees his Father doing. What the
Father does, the Son also does. This is because the Father loves the
Son. The Father shows him everything he does" (John 5:19–20).

Toward the end of his ministry, Jesus set his face to go to
Jerusalem, where he would die on a cross for our sins. Jesus knew
the hard road ahead, and in the Garden of Gethsemane the night
of his arrest, he asked God to spare him the suffering that was sure
to come. But Jesus submitted to his Father's will and stayed on the
right path.

Jesus went on to die on the cross and take our punishment. He
offers to exchange our poor record of sin with his perfect record of
righteousness. He lived a perfect life, saying no to the temptations to
walk the evil path. The writer of Hebrews explained it like this: "We
have a high priest who can feel it when we are weak and hurting.
We have a high priest who has been tempted in every way, just as
we are. But he did not sin" (Hebrews 4:15 NIrV).

If Jesus needed to go to his Father in prayer constantly, doesn't
it make sense that we need to pray constantly too?

Talk about It

▶ How was Jesus able to stay on the path of righteousness? *(Jesus
trusted his Father in heaven and filled his day with conversation with
him—what we call prayer.)*

▶ Can you think of a time when it was hard for you to stay on the right path? *(Parents help your children think of a time when it was difficult for them to follow the right path. Perhaps they needed to work hard on a school project when they would rather have played outside, or perhaps they had to trust God through a difficult circumstance or illness.)*

▶ Parents, share a time when you were tempted to stray from the right path and follow what you thought was right, rather than following God's Word? *(Think of an appropriate story from your life when you struggled to obey. Perhaps you knew God wanted you to ask forgiveness from your spouse, but in your mind you thought it would be OK to just forget about it. Or perhaps after thinking it was OK to tell a lie, God convicted you and you knew the right path was to tell the truth.)*

Pray about It

Thank Jesus for never straying off the righteous path. Ask him to help you follow him.

Week 5

God's Word

The Greatest Treasure

Day 1

Dig into the Word

Read Proverbs 2:1–5:

> *My son, if you will receive my words*
> *And treasure my commandments within you,*
> *Make your ear attentive to wisdom,*
> *Incline your heart to understanding;*
> *For if you cry for discernment,*
> *Lift your voice for understanding;*
> *If you seek her as silver*
> *And search for her as for hidden treasures;*
> *Then you will discern the fear of the* LORD
> *And discover the knowledge of God. (NASB)*

Have you ever dreamed of discovering a hidden treasure? What would it be like if you discovered a treasure map of your backyard hidden in a corner of your room under the carpet? Imagine following the directions on the map and starting to dig in your backyard at just the right spot. Imagine your excitement in finding a small wooden chest filled with gold coins. Wouldn't that make you want to search under all the carpets in your house?

The Bible may look like any other book on the outside, but inside it is full of treasure. You're probably not going to find a hidden treasure in your backyard, but if you dig into the Word of God, you are guaranteed to discover treasure.

God's Word is full of life-saving and life-giving truth. God's Word tells us who God is. It tells us how we should live. It tells us all about God's plan to save us from our sins so we can be forgiven.

Talk about It

▶ Did you ever think or dream about finding a treasure?

▶ Why do you think Proverbs compares searching God's Word to searching for a hidden treasure? *(The truth in the Bible is more valuable than gold. You can't take gold with you when you die, but all the valuable truth you learn in the Bible goes with you to heaven.)*

▶ Read Ephesians 2:4–9 and list some of the riches we have in Jesus. *(We have God's mercy, love, grace, and kindness. God has given us faith, salvation, and new life. We have been raised with Christ, we belong to him, we are seated with Christ in God's heavenly kingdom.)*

Pray about It

Ask God to make you excited to discover hidden treasure in the Bible.

 Day 2

Dig into the Word

Read Psalm 19:7–11:

> The law of the LORD is perfect, reviving the soul; the testimony of the LORD is sure, making wise the simple; the precepts of the Lord are right, rejoicing the heart; the commandment of the LORD is pure, enlightening the eyes; the fear of the LORD is clean, enduring forever; the rules of the LORD are true, and righteous altogether.

Follow the Directions

Supplies: brownie mix with directions covered; one dozen eggs; a bottle of oil; water in a pitcher; a box of salt; a canister of sugar; a packet of yeast; a variety of pans, bowls, and kitchen tools

The Bible doesn't claim to be a car repair manual to teach you how to change a flat tire, but it does give us everything we need to know how to

live. The Bible tells us who God is, who we are, and why God made us. As we read the Bible we get to know God better and better. We learn about how much God loves us. And the Bible teaches us all about how to love God and people—you could say that it is an instruction manual in love! The wise person reads and follows the Bible, but the fool rejects God's Word and tries to live life on his own. To see just how foolish rejecting God's Word is, try to make the brownies from the objects on the table without the help of the package directions (or other directions).

Now ask the kids for their ideas on how to prepare and bake the brownies. Write down the children's instructions. Then reveal the real instructions. Talk about how easy brownie making is when you follow the directions on the box instead of trying to figure things out for yourself. Explain that this is the same with God's Word. It tells us everything we need to know about God and how to love him and people.

More to be desired are they than gold, even much fine gold; sweeter also than honey and drippings of the honeycomb. Moreover, by them is your servant warned; in keeping them there is great reward.

God's Word gives us new strength, makes us wise, fills us with joy, teaches us how to live, and lasts forever. Obeying God's Word brings great reward.

Obeying God's Word sounds easy enough. Don't we just read it and do as it says? In Mark 10 we read about a man who knelt before Jesus and asked, "Good Teacher, what must I do to go to heaven?" Jesus's answer helps us to understand that we must do more than just obey a few commandments.

At first, Jesus asked the man if he knew the commandments like "Do not murder" and "Do not steal." The man replied, yes, he knew the commandments and had obeyed them from the time he was a little boy. Did Jesus congratulate him and say, "Well done! Of course you will go to heaven for your good work in obeying the commandments"? No, Jesus knew the man did not love God more than anything else. Jesus knew he was rich and loved his things most of all. So Jesus told the man to sell everything and follow him.

Instead of running to sell his possessions and follow Jesus, the man walked away sad. He had forgotten that the greatest commandment was to "love the Lord your God with all your heart and with all your soul and with all your mind" (Matthew 22:37).

Obeying God's Word is important, but the only way you can do that is by living for Jesus and loving him more than anything else. We can follow some of the rules, but still live for ourselves. But there is no way we can love Jesus with all our heart and also love money, the world, our success, or anything else with all our heart at the same time. God wants your whole heart.

Sing together
"Nuggets of Gold."

Chorus
Your Word's got nuggets of gold
A treasure for my soul
Getting them out is my goal
I'm gonna dig in, dig in, dig in
Like I'm diggin' for gold

Verse 1
I'll go exploring like a treasure hunter
Diggin' down deep in a mine
And Your Spirit's gonna help me discover
What I need to find

Verse 2
I'm gonna learn about the lazy sluggard
And to keep far away from the fool
I will see that pleasing God is much better
Than tryin' to be cool

Bridge
Your Word's got nuggets, nuggets of gold
Your Word's got nuggets, nuggets of gold
    (repeat)

Song
of the
Week

NUGGETS
OF GOLD

Music and words by David Fournier. © 2010 Sovereign Grace Worship (ASCAP). Sovereign Grace Music, a division of Sovereign Grace Churches. All rights reserved. Administrated worldwide at www.CapitolCMGPublishing. com, excluding the UK which is adm. by Integrity Music, part of the David C Cook family. www.SovereignGrace Music.org

From *Walking with the Wise*, http://www.sovereigngracemusic.org/Albums/Walking_with_the_Wise?pp=1|2

Talk about It

▶ In today's Scripture passage what words and phrases does the psalmist use to describe God's Word? *(God's Word is perfect, trustworthy, right, clear, pure, true, fair, valuable, and sweeter than honey. If your children are younger, reread the passage and have them raise their hands when they hear a word or phrase that describes God's Word. Older children can reread the passage for themselves.)*

▶ Reread the last sentence in today's Scripture. What will happen to us if we obey God's Word? *(We will receive a great reward.)*

▶ What reward is there for those who obey God's Word? *(The truth is that none of us can keep God's commandments perfectly. But, God's Word shows us Jesus, our Savior, is our reward both now and in the future.)*

Pray about It

Ask God to teach you how to love him more than anything else.

 Day 3

Dig into the Word

Read Proverbs 3:1–2:

> *My child, never forget the things I have taught you. Store my commands in your heart. If you do this, you will live many years, and your life will be satisfying. (NLT)*

Obedience to our parents is always good advice. In a perfect world, obedience to parents would bring a long and peaceful life. Even in this fallen world it is probably true that things go easier for the person who is willing to accept and follow the wisdom of more experienced people. But this proverb has deeper truth that is worth exploring.

Our world is not perfect; it is filled with sin, and sad things do happen. But if we belong to Jesus, we are a part of his kingdom and he has given us the job of working to bring his kingdom on earth. So what does this proverb mean to us who belong to God's kingdom? Well, look at Jesus. Where did obedience to God his Father get him? Did it get him a long and peaceful life? No, his life was brief and filled with conflict. What kind of relationship did Jesus have with his Father? Jesus says he never did anything apart from his Father's will. If that's the case, then it must have been God's will for Jesus, though perfectly obedient, to have a short and conflict-filled life. Jesus lived a sinless life and brought great joy to his Father in heaven. But don't forget that Jesus now lives forever in heaven with his Father. Now that is a long and satisfying life!

Obedience to our parents reflects a heart that is committed not to pleasing our parents, but to pleasing God. The blessings of obedience may indeed mean a long and peaceful life here on earth. What Proverbs is really talking about are spiritual blessings. God is pleased with our obedience, and the one who obeys becomes more like Christ and will live forever with Jesus in heaven.

Talk about It

▶ What two things does today's proverb tell us to do? *(Parents tell their children to remember what they have been taught and to obey their commands.)*

▶ Listening to parents and obeying can be difficult. Share a time when it was hard for you.

▶ If you have trouble obeying your parents do you also have trouble obeying God?

Pray about It

Ask God to help you remember and obey what the Bible and your parents tell you because that will be pleasing to your Father in heaven.

Day 4

Dig into the Word

Read Proverbs 19:16:

> *Keep the commandments and keep your life; despising them leads to death. (NLT)*

To despise something means to look down on something in a snooty way. It usually means that you think you don't need something or that you're too good for something. This proverb says that keeping the commandments is the way to life. Despising them is the way to death.

The problem is, even if we don't think we despise God's commandments, we still have no hope of obeying them perfectly. Does this mean the only thing we have to look forward to is dying? Absolutely not! That is exactly why Jesus came to earth and lived the perfect life we never could. Jesus obeyed God's commandments perfectly. Then on the cross he took the punishment—the death—we deserve.

Now he calls out to all of us to follow him. Anyone who admits their sin and turns away from it and trusts in Jesus is promised eternal life. Those who prefer to trust in themselves (thus despising what Jesus did) will die in their sin. Jesus said, "I am the resurrection and the life. Whoever believes in me, though he die, yet shall he live, and everyone who lives and believes in me shall never die" (John 11:25–26).

Talk about It

▶ How often do you disobey God? *(Parents, for starters, help your children think about how we love things more than God every day. Also share with them ways you disobey God every day.)*

▶ What is required to obey God's commandments perfectly? *(Perfect obedience requires a heart that is fully, completely committed to God every minute of every day for a whole lifetime.)*

▶ Why are we unable to perfectly obey God's commandments? What remedy has God provided for our sin? *(As long as we live, we will sin. The remedy for sin is found in Jesus's death on the cross.)*

Pray about It

Ask God to help you trust in Jesus for the forgiveness of your sin and for all of life.

 Day 5

Dig into the Word

Read John 1:1–5, 14, 18:

> *In the beginning the Word already existed. The Word was with God, and the Word was God. He existed in the beginning with God. God created everything through him, and nothing was created except through him. The Word gave life to everything that was created, and his life brought light to everyone. The light shines in the darkness, and the darkness can never extinguish it . . . So the Word became human and made his home among us. He was full of unfailing love and faithfulness. And we have seen his glory, the glory of the Father's one and only Son . . . No one has ever seen God. But the unique One, who is himself God, is near to the Father's heart. He has revealed God to us. (NLT)*

Proverbs 30:5 says: "Every *word* of God proves true; he is a shield to those who take refuge in him." What did the "Word" of God mean to the reader of the Old Testament? God's people knew that God acted through his words—that the world was created at his command—and that the word of God lasts forever (Psalm 33:6; Isaiah 40:8). Now that we have the New Testament we know that the Word of God is a person, God the Son—Jesus.

Jesus is the living Word who came down from heaven. When reading Proverbs, keep in mind the truth that Jesus is the Word. Jesus shows us God. For example, when we read, "Obey my words. Store up my commands inside you" (Proverbs 7:1 NIrV)), we need to remember that Jesus is God's Word and our greatest treasure. Remembering this helps us to think correctly about how to make the wisdom of Proverbs part of our everyday lives. In Proverbs we don't only have good advice, we have Jesus who is perfect Wisdom.

Talk about It

▶ Who is the Word of God? *(Jesus is the "Word" that became human—became a person—to live with us.)*

▶ What difference does it make that God's Word lives in you? *(Parents, talk about how God's living Word changes us, teaches us, convicts us, and encourages us.)*

▶ Share a Bible verse that has had an effect on you (changed you, taught you, convicted you, or encouraged you). *(Encourage your children to choose a favorite verse to memorize. That helps them personalize God's Word. Parents, come up with a favorite verse of your own.)*

Pray about It

Thank God for giving us Jesus, who helps us know him, know how to live, and know the way to be saved from our sins.

Week 6

Pay Attention

Learning to Follow Your Parents' Instruction

Day 1

Dig into the Word

Read Proverbs 1:8–9:

> *My child, listen when your father corrects you.*
> *Don't neglect your mother's instruction.*
> *What you learn from them will crown you with grace*
> *and be a chain of honor around your neck. (NLT)*

In this proverb, obedience to parents is pictured as a beautiful crown for our head and a lovely chain to wear as a necklace. That's like saying that obedience makes us look beautiful—like wearing jewelry makes someone look beautiful. The crown and necklace represent the godly character and blessing that come to you when you do what your parents tell you. That is why it is important to pay attention to what your parents say and "put on" or do what they ask.

There are two ways to listen to parents. The first way is to hear their words but then quickly forget them. The second way is to hear the words and then obey them. Imagine that your parents give you something beautiful to wear, but instead of wearing it, you leave it in the box and never put it on. That would be a waste of their gift.

In the same way, we must put on our parents' instructions. We do that by listening carefully to what they say and then following their instruction and advice. So if your mom tells you to speak respectfully to your teachers, you should do what she says. If your dad tells you to work hard until a job is done, you should listen and do your best to always finish a job. The only time we don't have to obey our parents or teachers is when they ask us to do something wrong.

Our obedience can't change our hearts. We can obey for the wrong reasons; for example, like boasting that you are better than your brother or sister. Only God can change our hearts so while you work to obey your parents, call out to God to help you obey for the right reasons.

Talk about It

▶ Recall a time when your parents gave an instruction that you quickly forgot about. *(Parents, share your own experience forgetting a parent's instruction.)*

▶ Can obeying our parents change our sinful hearts? *(No, only God can change our sinful heart into a heart that wants to obey out of love for God. But while we obey our parents on the outside, we can call out to God to change us on the inside.)*

▶ What if a parent or someone like a teacher asks you do something that is wrong? Do you still have to obey? *(You must follow God and his Word above all else. You do not need to obey someone who is telling you to do something the Bible says is wrong. If that should happen to you, please tell another adult you trust.)*

▶ Is it easy to obey your parents in everything? *(No, we need God's help to obey our parents. When we ask for help, God will give it to us.)*

Pray about It

Ask God to help you obey your parents and follow their instruction.

The Cooking Game

Supplies: recipe, list of ingredients

Select a recipe for a meal that requires multiple ingredients, e.g., meatloaf and mashed potatoes, lasagna, or chili. Make a list of all the ingredients (including herbs, spices, and condiments) required to prepare the meal. Do NOT show the list to your children.

Pull your children together and explain the Cooking Game. Tell them what you are going to have for dinner, e.g., lasagna. Explain that their job will be to collect from your pantry, fridge, or kitchen cabinets in five minutes everything required to make the dish. Have them put all the ingredients they are going to use—including salt and pepper, if required—onto a spot on your kitchen counter. Explain that once the game starts, you will not be able to answer any questions for five minutes.

After five minutes has passed tell them "time's up." Gather your kids together and explain how the kitchen is like life. It is full of good things to enjoy, but you need wisdom to make good choices and know how to put things together. Evaluate their

ingredients and let them know what they missed.

Tell them you are going to help them cook dinner and answer their questions about what is missing or what to do next. But explain that you will only answer their questions, if they first say, "(Mom or Dad) I need your wisdom to help me in life."

Adjust the exercise depending on the ages of your children. If they are younger, you can give them a few prompts, such as asking them what would be the first thing needed to make lasagna.

Answer any questions, produce the ingredient list, and offer help in finding whatever they can't locate.

As you prepare the meal, help your children understand how important your help will be for them in life. Encourage them to ask for your guidance and to listen to what you have to say. God has given children parents to help them make wise choices.

Day 2

Dig into the Word
Read Proverbs 7:1–3:

> *Follow my advice, my son; always treasure my commands. Obey my commands and live! Guard my instructions as you guard your own eyes. Tie them on your fingers as a reminder. Write them deep within your heart. (NLT)*

Our parents' teaching is precious, and we should protect it just as we protect and care for our eyes. Our eyes are delicate and precious and it is important that we protect them. That is why people wear safety glasses when they work with something that could fly back and hit them in the eye. This passage tells us that we should keep, or protect, God's commandments and our parents' teaching just as we would protect our eyes.

We keep God's Word and our parents' instruction by remembering it (writing it deep in our heart) and always being ready to put it into practice (binding it on our fingers).

Did you ever obey your parents but at the same time complain to yourself about them? For example, you want to play outside but your mom tells you to stay indoors because it's too rainy. You probably obey her, but what is going on inside your heart?

Or what if you and your sister get into a fight and Mom or Dad correct you and instruct you to forgive one another. Perhaps you say the words "I forgive you," but what is going on inside your heart?

God doesn't want us just to obey on the outside; he wants us to obey because we love him on the inside. Proverbs 23:26 says, "Give me your heart, and let your eyes observe my ways." It is important

Sing together
"All Ears."

Chorus
I wanna be all ears when Mom is speaking
All ears when Dad is teaching
There's a lot I don't know
And they've been around a whole lot of years
And have covered some ground
Their words will make me wise, so I'm all ears

Verse 1
When my eyes are tempted to wander away
I'll be all ears
When my mouth is jumping at something to say
I'll be all ears
Even when it's hard for me to hear

Verse 2
When my parents tell me that I should obey
I'll be all ears
When they teach me Jesus's loving ways
I'll be all ears
'Cause I know it's what I need to hear

Bridge
I've got two hands, two feet
Two elbows, two knees, but I'm all ears
Two eyes, one stare, and a whole lot of hair
But I'm all ears
Tomorrow, today, at school and at play
I'll be all ears
I'll be slow to speak, and quick to hear
'Cause I wanna be all ears!

Repeat Chorus.

to obey our parents on the outside, but obeying cannot just be an action. It must spring from a heart that is given to God.

Talk about It

▶ What does today's Scripture tell us to do with God's words and commandments? *(We are to treasure them, obey them, guard them, tie them, and write them.)*

▶ Can you think of a time when you got something in your eye? How important is it to protect your eyes? *(Parents draw out your children here to see if they remember a time when they got a speck in their eye. The object of this is to help them relate to how important it is to protect their eyes.)*

▶ How can you know whether or not you have given your heart to God? *(Help your children think about what motivates them in their obedience.)*

Pray about It

Ask God to show you your heart and to help you learn to love and cherish his Word.

 Day 3

Dig into the Word

Read Proverbs 4:1–5:

> *My children, listen when your father corrects you. Pay attention and learn good judgment for I am giving you good guidance. Don't turn away from my instructions. For I, too, was once my father's son, tenderly loved as my mother's only child. My father taught me, "Take my words to heart. Follow my commands, and you will live.*

Get wisdom; develop good judgment. Don't forget my words or turn away from them." (NLT)

Parents have had experiences in life that qualify them to give their children good advice. Take something as simple as throwing a ball inside a house. Most grown-ups have seen what can happen when a game meant to be played outside is played inside the house. They know that if you throw a ball outside and the ball hits a bush and knocks a few leaves off, it's no big deal. But if you throw a ball inside, it can shatter a treasured vase.

Children don't have the same life experience their parents do. It's hard for them to see the trouble that can result from their actions. For example, they think they can control the ball they throw inside the house. But as they get more excited, they lose control of the ball, and then it can fly anywhere!

You can learn two ways in life. You can learn by listening carefully to your parents and what they say (the "easy" way), or you can learn by making mistakes and feeling the sting of bad consequences (the "hard" way). Proverbs 12:15 says, "The way of the fool is right in his own eyes, but a wise man listens to advice."

If you have a hard time following the advice of people who are older and wiser than you, this might be telling you something about your heart. Are you teachable or are you stubborn? And take it a step further: do you let God teach you things? How hard is it for you to obey things you read in the Bible? These are things God can show you when you take an honest look at your heart.

Talk about It

▶ What is the difference between learning the "easy" way and learning the "hard" way? Why is learning the "easy" way sometimes not so easy? *(Learning the "easy" way is when we follow Proverbs and listen to instruction. It means we have to accept that others know better than we do. It requires being willing to listen and take direction from someone else. God calls this "humility.")*

▶ Can you remember a time when you or one of your siblings or friends had to learn by making mistakes themselves? *(Parents help draw out your children here. See if you can help them remember a time when someone learned a lesson the "hard" way.)*

▶ Can you remember a lesson your parents taught you that has helped you stay out of trouble? Why was it hard to accept their wisdom? *(Parents think about where your children are doing a good job listening to your advice. Use this as an opportunity to encourage them.)*

Pray about It

Ask God to help you listen carefully to your parents so that you can learn the joy of wisdom and avoid the trouble that comes from rejecting godly advice.

 Day 4

Dig into the Word

Read Proverbs 6:20–22:

> *My son, keep your father's commandment, and forsake not your mother's teaching. Bind them on your heart always; tie them around your neck. When you walk, they will lead you; when you lie down, they will watch over you; and when you awake, they will talk with you.*

Obeying your parents isn't always easy. We know the right thing to do, but too often we do the wrong thing anyway. Take losing your temper and getting angry, for example. We know we are not supposed to lose our temper. Our parents taught us not to yell, scream, and shout out angry words. But when we don't get what we want, anger can spring up quickly in our heart, and the next thing we know we are out of control, shouting at someone.

Jesus is the only person who obeyed his parents and the Lord's commandments all the time, every day.

Did you know that when we place our trust in Jesus God sends his Holy Spirit to live inside and help us obey? The Holy Spirit reminds us to follow Jesus and convicts us of our sin when we stray. In time, his work produces the fruit of the Spirit in our lives. The fruit of the Spirit, the apostle Paul tells us, is "love, joy, peace, patience, kindness, goodness, faithfulness, gentleness, and self-control" (Galatians 5:22–23).

Talk about It

▶ What do you think it means to tie something on your heart? *(Parents, draw out your children. Use the example of keeping keys on a key ring. The ring ties the keys together so they can't get lost. When we memorize God's Word and what our parents tell us, we are tying those words to our hearts to help us later.)*

▶ Why do you think obeying parents is so hard? *(Obeying is so hard because we want to do what we want to do, not what God wants us to do. Those "wants" draw us away from God.)*

▶ Who did Jesus send to help us after he returned to heaven? *(Jesus sent the Holy Spirit [see John 14:15–17].)*

Pray about It

Ask Jesus to help you recognize ways you try to be in charge and rebel against God as Lord of your life. Ask him to give you the Holy Spirit as your teacher.

Day 5

Dig into the Word
Read John 14:7–11:

> *"If you had known me, you would have known my Father also. From now on you do know him and have seen him." Philip said to him, "Lord, show us the Father, and it is enough for us." Jesus said to him, "Have I been with you so long, and you still do not know me, Philip? Whoever has seen me has seen the Father. How can you say, 'Show us the Father'? Do you not believe that I am in the Father and the Father is in me? The words that I say to you I do not speak on my own authority, but the Father who dwells in me does his works. Believe me that I am in the Father and the Father is in me, or else believe on account of the works themselves."*

The Bible tells us about a Father and a Son who love each other deeply. God the Father sent his Son Jesus to be born as a man. The Son of God obeyed his Father, laid aside his glory, and came to earth to live a perfect life and die on a cross for our sins.

Not only did Jesus obey his heavenly Father in everything, he obeyed his earthly father, Joseph, in everything too. Joseph worked as a carpenter and Jesus grew up helping to build things. Every time Joseph said, "Jesus, please bring me that chisel." Jesus obeyed. When Joseph directed Jesus to sweep the floor, he didn't stomp his foot in anger before he did what he was told. Jesus obeyed every time! This was really important. If Jesus had disobeyed his parents even once, his perfect life would be ruined and he would not have been able to take our sin and die for us as the perfect sacrifice. Even if Jesus had had one rebellious thought, he would not have been perfect any longer.

At his baptism, before Jesus began his adult ministry, God the Father called out from heaven and said, "This is my beloved Son, with whom I am well pleased."

We are all sinners from the time we are born. Not one of us has any hope of living a perfect life. But the good news is that Jesus lived our perfect life for us. When Jesus finished living his perfect life and died on the cross, he became the perfect sacrifice for our sin. The Bible tells us if we confess our sins and turn away from them and trust in Jesus, our sin is placed upon Jesus and we can be forgiven.

Talk about It

▶ Jesus had two fathers. Can you name them? *(Joseph was Jesus's father on earth and God the Father was his father in heaven.)*

▶ What did Jesus do that we are unable to do? *(Jesus obeyed God perfectly in everything.)*

▶ Why was it important that Jesus live a perfect life? *(Jesus had to live a perfect life so he could trade that perfect life for our sinful lives. Jesus didn't just die for our sin, he also lived a perfect life for us.)*

▶ Parents, did you obey your own parents when you were young? *(This is an opportunity to share your own struggles to obey and share how you needed God to change your heart. Try to think of an example that reveals deeper sin in your heart [for example, a time when you lied to make others think you were better than you were].)*

Pray about It

Thank Jesus for living a perfect life as a gift to everyone who believes in him and turns away from sin.

Week 7

We All Make Mistakes

Welcoming Correction

Day 1

....

Dig into the Word
Read Proverbs 15:5:

> *Only a fool despises a parent's discipline; whoever learns from correction is wise. (NLT)*

Last week we learned the importance of following our parents' instruction. This week's lesson is closely related. God gives us parents and teachers to help us learn. Being corrected when we make mistakes is part of learning. It is important that we learn to listen and obey their correction.

Sometimes correction comes with discipline. If you don't put your bike away when you are finished riding it, your parents might say you can't ride your bike the rest of the day. Discipline helps us realize how important it is to follow instructions. No one enjoys hearing that they did something wrong or need to be corrected. Still, correction and discipline help us to change. That is why Proverbs teaches us to welcome correction and not despise (hate) it. People who despise correction think they don't need it.

Welcoming correction sounds simple enough, but deep down we tend to think we know the best way to live. We think we can figure out our mistakes on our own. God knows we don't always see when we stray from the right path or listen to foolish advice. That is one reason he gives us parents and teachers.

Talk about It

▶ What does the word *correction* mean? *(Correction is about being set straight.)*

▶ What does the word *despise* mean? *(Despise is similar to hate, but it carries with it the sense that the despised thing is beneath you and you don't need it.)*

▶ Recall a time when you were corrected and got mad or annoyed. Try to describe what made you feel this way. *(Anger or annoyance when we are corrected shows a proud heart that thinks its own way is best.)*

Pray about It

Ask God to help you have a listening heart when you are corrected.

 Day 2

Dig into the Word

Read Proverbs 15:31–32:

> The ear that listens to life-giving reproof will dwell among the wise. Whoever ignores instruction despises himself, but he who listens to reproof gains intelligence.

Today's proverb brings a simple message: It is wise to listen to correction because it could save your life. Did you ever see this sign on a fence: "Danger of Electric Shock, Keep Out"? This message is not there just to give you a little information about the stuff behind the fence. The sign is actually a warning to anyone thinking of climbing the fence. Obeying the sign can save that person from an

Get It Straight

Supplies: a large photograph or painting hung on a wall at child's height, which can be adjusted to be straight or crooked on the wall

Take your child up to the picture hanging on a wall and have them close their eyes while you tilt it so that it is very crooked. Stand your child a foot away from the picture and ask them to straighten it on the wall. Once they think they have it straight, have them step back and see what it looks like. (It is very difficult to get a picture perfectly straight when you are close to it. If your child gets it correct, ask another member of your family to give it a try to illustrate the point, or you can "try" to straighten it yourself.)

Assuming your child didn't get the picture straight, have them stand close to it and adjust it while you give them directions from a distance, until the picture is perfectly level. Explain that trying to correct our own mistakes is like being the person close to the picture: you are sometimes too close to the situation to know how to get things straight. That is why we have God's Word and need others around us to speak into our lives.

electric shock. Our parents give life-giving warnings all the time: "Stop and look both ways before you cross the street" or "Don't play with fire." Parents know better than children how foolish and dangerous some choices can be. These warnings are life-giving because if you follow them, they can save your life.

The Bible is also filled with warnings—warnings that can save lives. Proverbs 11:19 says, "He who pursues evil will die." Ever since God warned Adam and Even not to disobey and eat the forbidden fruit, the punishment for sin has been death. That is still true for us today. Paul wrote, "The wages of sin is death, but the free gift of God is eternal life in Christ Jesus our Lord" (Romans 6:23). Sinners who refuse to run to Jesus for forgiveness will die in their sins and receive eternal punishment, but those who trust in Jesus, who died on the cross to take away our sins, will receive eternal life and live forever with Jesus.

When our parents warn or correct us with God's Word, it is not just to help us change our outward behavior. They correct us to point us to the way of Wisdom—to Jesus. The next time you are corrected, remember that God uses parents to help us find our way to him. If someone is really wise and understanding they know that God is the King of their life.

Talk about It

▶ What is the result of listening to warning and correction? (*Listening to warning and correction gives wisdom and understanding.*)

▶ Can you think of a time when a warning saved you from danger? (*Parents, help your children here. You might have told them not to run on a wet pool deck, or to wear a helmet while riding a bike. Think of some correction that helped prevent a life-threatening injury or consequence.*)

▶ "Those who turn away from correction hate themselves." What

Sing together
"I Don't Have to Hide"

Verse 1
When I have done something
I know I shouldn't do
And I'm tempted to hide it
When I have spoken words
I know I shouldn't speak
And I want to deny it
If I confess my sins, I'll find mercy

Chorus
Blessed is the one who fears the Lord
And admits his sin
Blessed is the one who trusts the Lord
Who alone forgives
Jesus died so I don't have to hide anymore

Verse 2
When I have taken something
I know I shouldn't take
And I try to conceal it
When I have disobeyed
The rules my parents made
I shouldn't keep it a secret
If I confess my sins, I'll find mercy

Bridge
When we know we're forgiven
We don't have to be afraid
We'll want to run from sin
And follow Jesus every day

Music and words by Zach Jones and Bob Kauflin. © 2010 Sovereign Grace Worship (ASCAP)/Sovereign Grace Praise (BMI). Sovereign Grace Music, a division of Sovereign Grace Churches. All rights reserved. Administrated worldwide at www.CapitolCMGPublishing.com, excluding the UK which is adm. by Integrity Music, part of the David C Cook family. www.SovereignGraceMusic.org

From *Walking with the Wise*, http://www.sovereigngracemusic.org/Albums/Walking_with_the_Wise?pp=1|2

do you think this means? *(If correction is a blessing and someone turns away from it, they must hate themselves.)*

Pray about It
Ask God to help you remember that correction is a blessing that God uses to draw you to himself.

 Day 3

Dig into the Word
Read Proverbs 10:17:

> *People who accept discipline are on the pathway to life, but those who ignore correction will go astray. (NLT)*

A young boy disobeyed his teacher. When it was time to stop playing after lunch and sit down to start the next class, the boy refused to sit down. After the teacher corrected him for his disobedience, the boy sat down, but as he took his seat he said, "I may be sitting down on the outside, but I'm standing up on the inside."

What he meant was that even though it looked like he was obeying, inside he was still stubborn and angry. Have you ever felt this way—angry and stubborn on the inside though you seemed to be obeying on the outside?

Jesus talked a lot about our hearts. He said: "You have heard that our ancestors were told, 'You must not murder. If you commit murder, you are subject to judgment.' But I say, if you are even angry with someone, you are subject to judgment!" (Matthew 5:21–22 NLT)

The people listening to Jesus had never murdered anyone. Because of this, they thought they were pretty good. Whenever they struggled with anger they excused their sin, thinking, *I'm not that bad. After all, I've never done anything as bad as murdering somebody.*

Jesus corrected them (and he corrects us too) by explaining that holding anger in your heart toward someone is the same sin as murder. Anger against someone is like a sinful seed that can grow into other sins like bitterness, hatred, and even murder.

Jesus knew that you can look good on the outside, but still hold anger on the inside, in your heart. And he knew that it was just as much a sin against God to disobey in your heart as in your behavior. That is why he taught so much about the heart. If you repent of (turn away from) sinful thoughts and confess them, they can't grow into sinful actions.

Talk about It

▶ To what serious sin did Jesus compare anger? (*Jesus compared the sin of anger to murder.*)

▶ Why is it important to turn away from anger while it is still only a sinful feeling in your heart? (*If you don't repent or turn away from sinful anger while it is in your heart, it can come out in angry actions that harm someone.*)

▶ Can you remember a time when angry feelings showed themselves in an outward sin, like hitting someone, or destroying someone's things? (*Parents, acting out anger is a more regular occurrence than kids may be aware of. Think of the young child who tosses her food off the table in anger, dirtying a clean floor. Or the child who in anger scribbles on his sibling's paper.*)

Pray about It

Ask God to help you receive Jesus's correction, and ask him to take away the anger in your heart.

Day 4

Dig into the Word

Read Proverbs 12:1:

To learn, you must love discipline; it is stupid to hate correction. (NLT)

The first step we take in receiving correction and discipline is to welcome it. Those who welcome correction soon realize that correction is helpful. Consider this: A mom asks her son if he would help by washing a pot in the sink, but the son has never washed a big pot before and starts to fill the pot with cold water. His mom sees and knows that it is a whole lot easier to wash a pot with hot water, so she corrects him. If the son is wise, he will listen to his mother's correction and use hot water, which makes the job so much easier.

The second step in receiving correction is to learn to "love" discipline and correction. We go after the things we love and don't just wait for them to come to us. Think of the boy washing the dishes again. When his mom corrects him for using cold water he thanks her and asks, "Is there anything else I should know?" Now he is not just welcoming correction, but he is asking for more of it because he knows how his mom's experience and wisdom can make the job easier.

Stupid is a word used to describe someone who lacks common sense and rejects knowledge. Sometimes we use the word *stupid* to poke fun at people's mistakes or to joke around. That is not kind. But in our Bible passage today, Solomon is not joking around. He is very serious and is trying to get our attention by using this harsh word to help us learn how important it is to welcome and love correction and discipline.

Talk about It

▶ How was the boy in the illustration helped by his mother's correction? (*It is a whole lot easier to wash a pot with hot water. It would have taken a lot longer to wash it clean in cold water.*)

▶ Can you think of a time when someone helped you by correcting you? (*Parents, help your children remember a time when you, a teacher, or a coach, helped them to grow through correction.*)

▶ Why should we love discipline when it can be painful? (*Discipline helps us to know there are consequences to our mistakes and teaches us to listen carefully the next time.*)

Pray about It

Ask God to help you always welcome instruction and correction.

 Day 5

Dig into the Word

Read Proverbs 3:11–12:

> My child, don't reject the LORD's discipline, and don't be upset when he corrects you. For the LORD corrects those he loves, just as a father corrects a child in whom he delights. (NLT)

Proverbs talks a lot about disciplining children. It's clear that God uses a parent's discipline and correction to teach children about walking on the path of Wisdom—on God's path.

Today's Scripture tells us a great truth about God: God is a Father who loves his children. God disciplines us to help us see our sin. Once we see that we are sinners, separated from God, we know we need a Savior. And God so loved the world that he gave his only

Son Jesus to be our Savior. Jesus lived the perfect life we could not live, and then died to take the punishment for our sins.

The true path of life leads us to Jesus. Every other path leads us astray. That is why when parents discipline us, or when God allows hard things, it is all out of love to keep us pointed in God's direction. The evil and wrong paths of this world lead away from God. Those who go in the wrong direction want us to believe we don't need God—that we can get along fine without him. But that is a lie and God's discipline, while painful, is designed to keep us on the right path and lead to life in Jesus.

Talk about It

▶ Why does God discipline us? (*God disciplines us because he loves us.*)

▶ Read Hebrews 12:1–7. Who does the writer of Hebrews tell us we are to look to as we run the race of life? (*Jesus is the one we are to look to.*)

▶ How have the hard things in your life helped to keep you looking to Jesus? (*Parents share a time when God brought a trial into your life that drew you closer to him.*)

Pray about It

Ask God to help you see how discipline is a sign of his love.

Week 8

Looking to the Ants

Learning Diligence

Day 1

Dig Into the Word

Read Proverbs 6:6–11:

> *Go to the ant, O sluggard; consider her ways, and be wise. Without having any chief, officer, or ruler, she prepares her bread in summer and gathers her food in harvest. How long will you lie there, O sluggard? When will you arise from your sleep? A little sleep, a little slumber, a little folding of the hands to rest, and poverty will come upon you like a robber, and want like an armed man.*

Or here's another way to say it:

> *Take a lesson from the ants, you lazybones. Learn from their ways and become wise! Though they have no prince or governor or ruler to make them work, they labor hard all summer, gathering food for the winter. But you, lazybones, how long will you sleep? When will you wake up? A little extra sleep, a little more slumber, a little folding of the hands to rest—then poverty will pounce on you like a bandit; scarcity will attack you like an armed robber. (NLT)*

God gave Solomon the wisdom to study the animals that lived around him. Solomon drew lessons from the animals' lives, knowing it was God who created them. The Bible tells us that Solomon knew all about the beasts of the field, the birds of the air, reptiles, and the fish (1 Kings 4:33). Solomon also watched insects and learned from them.

Imagine watching a column of ants, each carrying a morsel of food, creeping across the ground single file back to their colony. If you look closely, you can see that the ants have something to teach people—especially lazy people. God created ants to work, and God created man to work. God gave Adam and Eve the job of caring for creation. So work is a good thing that God created.

As today's passage points out, laziness leads to bad consequences. Wanting to avoid bad consequences is one reason for not being lazy. But it's not the biggest reason.

The big reason is this: As God's children, we are God's hands and feet to the world. God has given his children the job of ruling over creation. So it's our calling from God to work hard at everything he has given us to do. We honor God as we work for him.

In Colossians 3:17 we read, "And whatever you do, in word or deed, do everything in the name of the Lord Jesus, giving thanks to God the Father through him." This means that whatever we do—whether it's studying, cleaning, working in an office, cooking, building—we should do it as for the Lord. As children of God, our work is holy.

Talk about It

▶ What lessons can we learn from the ants? *(They work diligently, and they don't have to be told what to do.)*

▶ What would your life look like if you lived like an ant every day? *(Parents, help your children connect the lesson to their daily lives. If they lived like an ant they would clean their room without being told, get their schoolwork and chores done on time, and ask to help with*

Coin Sorting Machine

Supplies: a stopwatch or timer, loose change (30 pennies, 30 nickels, 30 dimes, and 30 quarters), and four bowls. This exercise works for three to four people.

Explain that a diligent person is someone who carefully and completely finishes a job on time. A lazy person, on the other hand, is slow to finish, does only enough work to get by, and doesn't care if the job is not completely finished.

The goal of today's game is to separate the coins like a change-counting or coin-sorting machine. Each person is responsible for one or two of the four coin types. (If you have three people, eliminate one of the coin types.)

Have all players seated around a table and set the bowls in front of the players. Divide the coins equally among the players and place their mixed set of coins in the bowl in front of them. Then assign each person a particular coin type to collect.

When you start the game, players begin by picking up one coin at a time from their bowl. If the coin they pick matches the type they were assigned to collect, they stack the coin on the table in front of them. If it does not match, they drop it in the bowl of the person to their right. Use the stopwatch to time how long

it takes for everyone, working as a team, to sort and stack all the coins.

Now do the exercise again, only this time, assign one person to be the "sluggard." This person should take a break (by counting slowly to ten) after every five coins they pick up. Talk about how much the game was affected when one person played the sluggard.

Finally, play the game again without the sluggard, and see if you can beat your original time.

extra work around the house. The other thing that ants do is they work until a job is finished. If you watch ants outside, you will never see one take a break while there is still work to be done.)

▶ Explain the big reason for working hard at what we do. *(God has given us jobs to do, and we should do them well because we work for him.)*

Pray about It

Thank God for giving us an important job to do in his kingdom.

 Day 2

Dig into the Word

Read Proverbs 24:30–34:

> *I passed by the field of a sluggard, by the vineyard of a man lacking sense, and behold, it was all overgrown with thorns; the ground was covered with nettles, and its stone wall was broken down. Then I saw and considered it; I looked and received instruction. A little sleep, a little slumber, a little folding of the hands to rest, and poverty will come upon you like a robber, and want like an armed man.*

The book of Proverbs often teaches the same lesson more than once to make sure we don't miss it or forget. The sluggard in today's Scripture reading has been lazy for a long time. Thorns have overgrown his rows of grapes, which means he has not weeded his vineyard. Instead of cutting the grass between the rows of vines, the sluggard has allowed weeds like nettles to grow unhindered. Nettles are plants with prickles that sting you when you touch them. What's more, the vineyard wall is broken down. The wall protects

Sing together
"Lazy Bones."

Song
of the
Week

LAZY
BONES

Verse 1
Have you heard about Mr. Lazy Bones?
You can find him sleeping on his couch at home
When there's work outside for him to do
He is working hard to find another excuse

Verse 2
Mr. Lazy Bones tells you he's afraid
Never ever finishes the plans he's made
When you want his help around the house
You can try to find him but he's never around

Chorus
Lazy Bones can help us see
What we never want to be
He doesn't have a hope or a clue
When we work to please the Lord
God will make our plans secure
And He'll be glorified in all we do

Verse 3
See the busy ants working all the time
No one has to tell them how to stay alive
Getting ready for winter days ahead
Gathering their food until the time comes to rest

Music and words by Doug Plank, Stephen Altrogge, and Bob Kauflin. © 2010 Sovereign Grace Worship (ASCAP)/Sovereign Grace Praise (BMI). Sovereign Grace Music, a division of Sovereign Grace Churches. All rights reserved. Administrated worldwide at www.CapitolCMGPublishing.com, excluding the UK which is adm. by Integrity Music, part of the David C Cook family. www.SovereignGraceMusic.org

From *Walking with the Wise*, http://www.sovereigngracemusic.org/Albums/Walking_with_the_Wise?pp=1|2

the fruit on the vines from hungry animals and thieves. If there are any grapes, they are likely to be eaten or stolen before the harvest.

Before you are too critical of the sluggard in the story, compare your bedroom to the vineyard. Do you have dirty clothes scattered on your floor like weeds? Do you have things lying around where they can be tripped over? Is your bed unmade? Do you leave dirty dishes and half-eaten food lying around to attract insects and rodents?

The sluggard in the story didn't ruin his vineyard in one day. He could catch up with his chores if he missed a few days' work. However, the sluggard fools himself into thinking he can rest day after day after day. In the end, poverty sneaks up on him to rob him of his crop. Without grapes to harvest and sell, the sluggard will have no money to buy food.

Talk about It

▶ Was it wrong for the sluggard in the story to take a break? *(The sluggard's problem wasn't that he took a break. His problem was that he didn't work. Sloth deceives us into thinking we can keep taking breaks.)*

▶ What should the vineyard owner in today's story have done differently? *(He should have repaired the wall and weeded his grapevines.)*

▶ Is there an area of your life that is kind of like the sluggard's vineyard? *(Parents, help your children think of the messy areas of their lives like their bedroom, bathroom, backpack, or school notebook.)*

Pray about It

Ask God to help you work diligently.

Day 3

Dig into the Word

Read Proverbs 10:2–5:

> *Ill-gotten gains do not profit, But righteousness delivers from death. The LORD will not allow the righteous to hunger, But He will reject the craving of the wicked. Poor is he who works with a negligent hand, But the hand of the diligent makes rich. He who gathers in summer is a son who acts wisely, But he who sleeps in harvest is a son who acts shamefully. (NASB)*

Did you catch all that? Here's another way of saying it.

> *Riches that are gained by sinning aren't worth anything. But doing what is right saves you from death. The LORD gives those who do right the food they need. But he lets those who do wrong go hungry. Hands that don't want to work make you poor. But hands that work hard bring wealth to you. A child who gathers crops in summer is wise. But a child who sleeps at harvest time brings shame. (NIrV)*

Do you know what a backdrop is? A backdrop is used on an acting stage. It is a large flat canvas painted with a background scene. The action takes place in front of the backdrop. If many trees are painted on the backdrop, it will appear to the audience like the actors are walking through a forest. When we read the book of Proverbs, it is important that we remember that it too has a backdrop—something we see behind the bits of wisdom.

Today's Bible passage gives wisdom about diligence and work. Notice, however, that the lessons listed here contain *common sense* wisdom. You don't have to be a Christian to agree that you should work honestly or that if you work hard your family will be proud of you. So what makes these proverbs Christian? This is where the backdrop comes in.

The backdrop to Proverbs is God's kingdom and God's glory. When Proverbs talks about riches, it's talking about spiritual riches, not earthly riches. When Proverbs talks about satisfaction, peace, or rewards, it's talking about spiritual satisfaction, spiritual peace, and spiritual reward. The wisdom of Proverbs cannot be separated from the fact that as Christians our whole purpose is to work for God's glory. God is the King and it is for him and his kingdom that we work.

The apostle Paul wrote, "So, whether you eat or drink, or whatever you do, do all to the glory of God" (1 Corinthians 10:31). So when we read "the hand of the diligent makes rich," remember this is about being diligent to glorify God, not ourselves. When we read, "he who gathers in summer is a prudent son," remember that we are not just working to please our earthly parents, but also our Heavenly Father. Living for God's glory should be the backdrop behind everything we do.

Talk about It

▶ What do think it means to work for God's glory? *(When we work for God's glory, we keep in mind that our goal is to please God.)*

▶ Is it possible to be diligent for yourself and not for God? Can you give an example? *(Plenty of people work hard to get rich for themselves and don't care about God at all.)*

▶ What can you do to bring glory to God? *(Parents, help your children think through areas of their lives where they can demonstrate diligence, but do it to honor and glorify God.)*

Pray about It
Ask God to help you remember that your goal is to bring glory to him.

 Day 4

Dig into the Word
Read Colossians 3:23:

> *Whatever you do, work heartily, as for the Lord and not for men.*

God is pleased when we work hard and keep working hard. But God is also interested in why we are working. The Bible tells us that God isn't only looking at what we do; he is looking at our attitude about what we do. He wants us to do each job with our whole heart to bring him glory.

Did you ever see someone who is working hard with a not-very-good attitude? Perhaps you remember a time when you couldn't go out to play because you had to clean your room. Maybe you cleaned your room, but did it with a bad attitude. Even though it looked like you were obeying, you were really, in your heart, going against God.

Or maybe you did some yard work for a neighbor, but complained the whole time about how demanding and picky your neighbor was about raking leaves. This is not what God desires. He wants us to work as if he is our boss.

Some people work hard to look good and gain the attention of others. But this is not how God wants us to work. He wants us to work hard for *his* glory, not our own.

Talk about It

▶ Think about the last job or chore you had to do. Did you work as if God was your boss?

▶ How would having the attitude that you are working for the Lord change how you view your chores?

▶ Why do you think God wants us to work for his glory?

Pray about It

Ask God to help you work hard for his glory.

 Day 5

Dig into the Word

Read Ephesians 2:8–9:

> *For by grace you have been saved through faith. And this is not your own doing; it is the gift of God, not a result of works, so that no one may boast.*

Hard work and diligence are important to God. God includes work as part of the commandment to rest. God tells us, "Six days you shall work, but on the seventh day you shall rest." God created work for Adam and Eve before they sinned, so we know that work is a good thing.

But even though work is important and good for us, our work can never save us. Even the most diligent person in the world cannot work hard enough to pay for their sin. The only way we get to heaven is through Jesus and his work. Jesus lived a perfect life in our sinful world and then died on the cross so that we could be forgiven. By his life, death, and rising from the dead, Jesus is able to offer us forgiveness. As sinners, we can't work our way back to a perfect life. But we don't have to. Jesus gives us his perfect life for free. We can't brag or boast that we earned our way to heaven, for it is all grace, by the work of Jesus. When we work hard, we are thanking God for his mercy and grace.

Talk about It

▶ What does the word *grace* mean in today's Scripture passage? *(Grace means free gift.)*

▶ What work did Jesus do to open a way into heaven? *(Jesus lived a perfect life and died on the cross to pay the penalty we deserved.)*

▶ Why should we work hard to obey God if forgiveness and heaven are a free gift that we can't work for? *(We don't work hard to earn God's love; we work hard to say thank you to God for his grace. Imagine how grateful a person would be to a doctor who saved him from a terrible disease. How much more grateful are we to God for saving us from sin!)*

▶ When did you first understand that salvation was a free gift to you from God? *(Share your testimony and let your kids know when you realized you needed to trust in Jesus, his perfect life, and sacrifice on the cross.)*

Pray about It

Thank God for what he did to save you. Ask him to help you remember this and work hard, not for your own glory but for his.

Week 9

A Generous Heart

Learning to Give

Day 1

Dig into the Word

Read Proverbs 3:9–10:

> *Honor the LORD with your wealth and with the first-fruits of all your produce; then your barns will be filled with plenty, and your vats will be bursting with wine.*

Did you know that God created everything and owns everything?

▶ Colossians 1:16 says, "All things were created through him and for him."

▶ God says, "For every beast in the forest is mine. The cattle on a thousand hills. I know all the birds in the hills and all that moves in the field is mine" (Psalm 50:10–11).

▶ Psalm 24:1 says, "The earth belongs to the LORD. And so does everything in it. The world belongs to him. And so do all those who live in it" (NIrV).

Today's Scripture teaches us to give an offering back to God from our "firstfruits." A "firstfruit" might seem like a strange phrase, but it just means to give to God before we give to anyone else (even ourselves!), as a way of remembering that everything we have belongs to God. Of course God doesn't need anything from us. But giving to God is a way that we honor him and show our love to him. In the time that Proverbs was written, if a farmer grew wheat, he gave God an offering from the first of the harvest. If he raised lambs, his offering might be from the firstborn lambs.

Today, we also give to God to honor him and help us to remember that everything we have and are comes from him. What might be some of the "firstfruits" your family could give to God? For your family a "firstfruit" might be the money you give to your church and missionaries or it might mean time you spend helping others with the gifts and talents God has given you. It doesn't matter if you don't have a lot of money to give—there is always something you can do that will honor God.

In the Old Testament, God told his people to honor him by giving back a tithe, or a tenth of everything they received to honor him (Malachi 3:10). God's people still give a percentage of what they make back to God today. Many people give more than ten percent. That's one way we help to spread the gospel throughout the whole world—by supporting churches, missions, and ministries that point others to God.

In today's reading from Proverbs, we are reminded that God will bless us abundantly when we give. That doesn't mean we will get a lot of money from God! It means that God will bless us with the spiritual blessing of becoming generous like he is. You simply can't out give God. If you think about it, he has already given you everything you have.

Talk about It

▶ What are the firstfruits? *(Think of a fruit grower, picking his fruit. The firstfruits would be the first basket of ripe fruit that comes from his tree. If a farmer thought his apple trees would yield ten baskets of apples, the first basket of the ten would be the firstfruits of the harvest. The Bible tells us to give God the firstfruits as an offering.)*

A Secret Gift

Supplies: a one- five- ten- or twenty-dollar bill, a blank note card

Tell your children this week's lesson is about the value of generosity and that you are going to start the week by giving someone a secret gift to bless them. Show them the money and the note card. Explain that you are going to first choose who should receive the gift. Select someone in need or simply someone you want to bless. Each person will get a chance to write something in the card.

After you discuss who to give the secret gift to, give each of your children a chance to draw a picture or write an encouragement in the card. Remember, if it is to be a secret gift, you can't sign your names.

Address the card, put the money in, and seal the envelope. Then take time to pray that God would use your secret gift to encourage and bless the recipient. Talk with your family about how it felt to give and how giving brings a double blessing. The person who receives the gift is blessed, but so is the giver.

▶ What is Proverbs encouraging everyone to do to honor the Lord? *(Proverbs is encouraging everyone to give God an offering from their firstfruits. That is, give the Lord an offering before we spend our money on ourselves.)*

▶ Since not many of us are farmers, what does it look like for us to give from our firstfruits? *(We can give from the money we receive for working. So if you help your mom around the house and she gives you ten dollars, you can give the first dollar you spend back to God as an offering of thanks. If you are not working yet, you can also give your time to help others—perhaps babysitting at church, or working to clean your church. Another way is to use your talents to honor God.)*

Pray about It

Thank God for giving you all that you have. Ask him to help you be generous with everything you have. Remember, it is not about how much you have. The widow who only had two copper coins and placed them in the offering was commended by Jesus (Matthew 12:41–44).

 Day 2

Dig into the Word

Read Proverbs 21:5–6:

> *The plans of the diligent lead surely to abundance, but everyone who is hasty comes only to poverty. The getting of treasures by a lying tongue is a fleeting vapor and a snare of death.*

Read Matthew 6:21:

> *For where your treasure is, there will your heart be also.*

**Sing together
"A Generous Heart."**

Chorus
God loves a generous heart, a generous heart
Yes, He does
God loves a generous heart, a generous heart
Cause that's a heart like His own heart
That's a heart like His own

Verse 1
There are those who give away
It seems the more they give,
   the more they gain
There are others who hold back
The more they try to keep,
   the more they lack
The more they lack

Verse 2
God has shown us how to give
He offered up His Son so we might live
Jesus gave His precious blood
To wash us clean and bring us back to God
Back to God

Bridge
We can't out give God
For He's the Giver of life and every good thing
We can't out give God
He just keeps pouring out more
He's the wonderful King!

Music and words by Mark Altrogge. © 2010 Sovereign Grace Praise (BMI). Sovereign Grace Music, a division of Sovereign Grace Churches. All rights reserved. Administrated worldwide at www.CapitolCMGPublishing.com, excluding the UK which is adm. by Integrity Music, part of the David C Cook family. www.SovereignGraceMusic.org

From *Walking with the Wise*, http://www.sovereigngracemusic.org/Albums/Walking_with_the_Wise?pp=1|2

Yesterday we learned that all we are and have belongs to God and comes from God. Today we learn that there is a right way and a wrong way to gain riches, and it all starts with what is most important to us (what we treasure the most).

Proverbs talks a lot about money (as does the rest of the Bible). Solomon and others who wrote Proverbs knew that some people will do just about anything to get money—lie, steal, and cheat. Why is that so? Because their "treasure" is money and the things money can buy. It's true that if you lie, steal, and cheat you can sometimes get more money than by being honest. And that can feel like fun. But the pleasure goes away quickly, like a vapor or a wisp of smoke fading into the air. Once you spend the money you gained by lying, it is gone. But your sin remains, and one day you will have to answer to God for what you did (and you might have to answer to the people you cheated as well)!

When people become followers of Jesus, they begin to treasure their relationship with God more than money. Because their hearts change, that means they change the way they think about their money. Often that means changes to how they spend their money. Mary, for example, poured her expensive perfume on Jesus's feet (John 12:3). Zacchaeus gave half of what he owned to the poor (Luke 19:8). The new believers in the early church shared all that they owned so that no one was in need (Acts 2:44-45), and Barnabas sold land and gave all the money to the apostles (Acts 4:37). Once these people saw Jesus as their greatest treasure, it changed the way they looked at earthly riches. When we give our hearts and lives in service to God, he changes the way we look at earthly treasure too.

Talk about It

▶ What is a lying tongue? *(A person who does not tell the truth is said to have a lying tongue.)*

▶ Can you think of a way a person with a lying tongue could gain money dishonestly? *(Parents, see if your children can think of a different example than those listed. Another example: they could ask for a second cookie and lie when asked if they already ate one.)*

▶ Why would somebody lie to get more of something? *(When we love something more than God, we want more of it and will do anything to get it.)*

Pray about It
Ask God to help you love him most of all, more than the things of the world.

 Day 3

Dig into the Word
Read Proverbs 11:24–25:

> *One gives freely, yet grows all the richer; another withholds what he should give, and only suffers want. Whoever brings blessing will be enriched, and one who waters will himself be watered.*

Also read Acts 20:35:

> *It is more blessed to give than to receive.*

God is the great giver and when he makes you his child it becomes your joy to give also. Proverbs 11:24–25 and Acts 20:35 are really saying the same thing—in giving to others we are like our heavenly Father, who gives us everything we have. The blessing comes in knowing that giving with a generous heart makes us like our heavenly Father. Doesn't it make you happy to know you are being like God?

How does God give to us? Just as the passage from Proverb says,

God gives to his children *freely*. God the Father sent his one and only Son to this world to die for the sins of his people. He gave us his greatest treasure. Jesus freely left heaven and gave up his life for all who believe. What greater gift could we have ever been given?

Proverbs tells us that we are to imitate God and freely give our most treasured possessions to bless others. When we give freely, God will bless us—not usually with more money, but with the much bigger blessing of becoming more like him. If you hold back what God has given you, you also miss out on the joy of giving to others. When we share with others what we have—our time, our food, our homes, our money, our concern—we get to see the joy our giving brings into their lives. That, in turn, brings us joy.

Did you ever notice people like to give to people who give? If someone gives your family a Christmas card or gift, it makes you want to bless them back and give them a card. If someone shares their lunch with you when you have none, it makes you want to look for a way to bless them when they are in need. Cheerful giving is catching! The apostle Paul wrote in the New Testament that "God loves a cheerful giver" (2 Corinthians 9:7). So if you are generous and cheerfully give to others, you will gain their thanks, but even more importantly you will be doing the exact thing that God loves!

Talk about It

▶ Recall a time when you experienced how it is more blessed to give than to receive.

▶ If giving brings joy and blessing, why are people unwilling to give? *(Parents, this is another opportunity to help your children see how we are so often tempted to think only of ourselves. We need God's help to do what is right.)*

▶ What blessings has God given you that you can share? *(Think about how you can use your time or possessions or money or health and strength to give to others.)*

Pray about It

Ask God to give you a generous heart so that you can pass on to others the blessings he pours out on you.

 Day 4

Dig into the Word

Read Proverbs 11:28:

> *Whoever trusts in his riches will fall, but the righteous will flourish like a green leaf.*

Solomon was the richest man who ever lived. He owned huge amounts of gold and even more silver. Solomon's ships brought back tons of gold and fine goods (1 Kings 9:26–28). Other rulers and kings brought loads of gold and good things (1 Kings 10:25). The Bible tells us that Solomon received more than six hundred talents of gold each year (1 Kings 10:14). A talent weighs seventy-five pounds. Today gold is worth more than $1200 per ounce. There are twelve hundred ounces in just one talent, which is worth a million and a half dollars. Solomon got more than six hundred talents each year! That means every year Solomon received a billion dollars worth of gold! But Solomon kept the gold for himself. Instead of blessing the people of God, he treated them harshly and taxed them to get even more money (1 Kings 12:4).

Solomon did build a costly temple for God, but it didn't cost him anything. His father King David and the people of Israel gave sacrificially of their own money to pay for the construction. King David gave three thousand talents of gold, worth over four billion dollars today, from his own money (1 Chronicles 29:3–4). When the people of Israel saw his generosity, they also gave five thousand talents of gold worth seven billion dollars today.

On top of that, they offered silver, precious stones, and other gifts. Solomon should have followed their example. But instead of sharing with the people of Israel, Solomon used his money to build himself a great palace and to build cities to store all the chariots and horses that he bought.

Both David and his son Solomon were sinners, but one big difference showed when King David was caught in sin and turned to God and said he was sorry (see Psalms 32 and 51). That's why David can be called "righteous." Anyone who puts their faith in God and turns from their sin will "flourish like a green leaf" because Jesus gives us his righteousness.

It does seem from the end of Ecclesiastes that Solomon turned to God at the end of his life, but because he loved the things of the world more than God, his kingdom was taken from his son and most of what he gained was lost.

Talk about It

▶ How was King David different than Solomon his son in how they handled their riches? *(King David gave up his riches for the building of the temple. Solomon trusted in his riches and kept them for himself.)*

▶ How was Jesus different from Solomon? *(Jesus gave up everything for his Father in heaven and for us. He gave up his heavenly throne to be born a poor man and then died on the cross for our sins.)*

▶ What do you think the Lord wants us to do with everything he gives us? *(God wants us to use everything we have for his glory.)*

Pray about It

Ask God to give us generous hearts that are motivated to give because of how much God has given us.

Day 5

Dig into the Word

Read John 3:16–17:

> *For God so loved the world, that he gave his only Son,*
> *that whoever believes in him should not perish but have*
> *eternal life. For God did not send his Son into the world*
> *to condemn the world, but in order that the world might*
> *be saved through him.*

Jesus is the most valuable gift ever given. To save us from our sin, God the Father gave us his only Son. The Son of God left his throne in heaven and was born as a helpless baby in a stable. Jesus was rejected by his people, abandoned and betrayed by his closest friends, mocked, beaten, and nailed to a cross where he took our punishment. God the Father gave his only Son; Jesus gave his life. Jesus knew what it was like to give up the treasures of heaven to obey and serve his Father.

We must make a choice in life. Are we going to serve God and place our trust in the Son he gave to take away our sin, or are we going to place our trust in getting a lot of money and things? Jesus knew that you can't serve both God and money at the same time (Matthew 6:24). The reason we cannot serve both God and money is because they present opposite goals for our lives. God calls us to give our earthly treasure away and seek heavenly treasure, while money calls us to seek earthly treasure and keep it for ourselves.

Jesus said it like this: "Don't store up treasures here on earth, where moths eat them and rust destroys them, and where thieves break in and steal. Store your treasures in heaven, where moths and rust cannot destroy, and thieves do not break in and steal.

Wherever your treasure is, there the desires of your heart will also be" (Matthew 6:19–21 NLT).

So what is "treasure in heaven"? Our treasure in heaven is not a thing, like a gold bar or a diamond ring. Our treasure is a person, Jesus Christ. If money is our most important treasure, we will serve money and make earning a lot of it our most important goal. But if Jesus is our greatest treasure, then we will live for him.

Talk about It

▶ What is the greatest gift ever given? *(God's Son Jesus is the greatest gift ever given.)*

▶ Why did God give us his only Son? *(God gave us his only Son because he loved us and because there was no other way for him to have a relationship with us.)*

▶ Why can't we serve both God and money? *(We only have room in our heart for one love. If we live for money, we will make choices to get and keep money. But if we live for God, we will make choices to get and keep God. Serving God and serving money are very different.)*

▶ Parents, share a time when you made a decision to serve God rather than money. *(Talk about your giving to the church, or share a story about a time when God led you to give money to someone in need, even though you could have enjoyed keeping the money for yourself.)*

Pray about It

Thank God for the greatest gift of all—for sending his Son Jesus to die on the cross for our sins. Ask him to help you live for Jesus.

Week 10

Good Company

Becoming a True Friend

Day 1

Dig into the Word
Read Proverbs 13:20:

Whoever walks with the wise becomes wise, but the companion of fools will suffer harm.

Friends have an effect on one another. The more time we spend with someone, the more we act like them, and talk like them and the more they act and talk like us. If we hang out with foolish people, sooner or later we will be led into foolishness. But if we hang out with wise friends, they will lead us to wisdom.

The most important question we need to ask when choosing a friend is "Do they love God?" The Bible warns us, "The fool says in his heart, 'There is no God.'" It is one thing if a friend does something foolish, like wearing his good clothes to play tackle football. We all make foolish mistakes in life. It is far worse and far more foolish if one of your friends is trying to draw you away from God.

It's OK to be friends with someone who doesn't know God. After all, we all start out as unbelievers until we place our trust in Jesus. One of the best ways to be a friend is to tell someone about God and how wonderful he is. But it is not wise to remain a friend of someone who regularly tempts you to walk away from God and go down the wrong path.

Talk about It

▶ What kind of friends does Proverbs encourage us to walk with? *(Proverbs tells us to choose wise friends.)*

▶ What kind of things should we look for in a wise friend? *(A wise friend is faithful and helps you grow closer to God. He does not pull you away from God.)*

▶ What can happen if you choose friends who try to get you to go down the wrong path or make sinful choices? *(They could lead you away from God to walk on a sinful path. The consequences of that would be harmful.)*

Pray about It

Ask the Lord to make you a wise person who loves him. Ask God to give you wise friends who love him too.

 Day 2

Dig into the Word

Read Proverbs 22:24–25:

> *Do not associate with a man given to anger; Or go with a hot-tempered man, Or you will learn his ways And find a snare for yourself. (NASB)*

Once again we see that the behavior of our friends rubs off on us. The more you play around fire, the more you smell like smoke. It is the same way with friends. If you hang around friends who have bad habits, sooner or later you are going to learn their bad behavior. It is also important to remember that each of us is a friend to someone.

The Blind Leading the Blind

Supplies: three people, two blindfolds, a few obstacles (chairs work well)

Set some chairs up randomly in a room. Blindfold two people. Explain that the first blindfolded person should lead the second across the room, avoiding the obstacles. Spin both individuals around to help confuse them and have them face one another. Act as a safety spotter as they make their way through the course.

Do the exercise again, switching leader/follower. Then have them do it a third time, this time removing the blindfold from the leader.

Discuss how much easier it was to follow a guide who could see. Connect this to life by explaining the importance of choosing friends who can help us see a way through life's troubles. We want to choose friends who trust God's Word so that we can go to them for godly advice.

Our wrong choices can lead them astray as well.

On top of that, we are not always able to see our own weaknesses. Hunters hide traps called snares, which are wire loops that catch a foot of an unsuspecting animal. The harder the animal fights to get away, the tighter a snare holds it. Good friends help each other by pointing out these blind spots, like anger, so that we don't get snared in sin. We all get angry from time to time, and we can help each other by correcting one another (remember we talked about that in week 7). Then we repent and confess our anger before it grows into a trap to catch others.

And it is always good to remember that when we confess our sins to God, he promises to help us change (1 John 1:9).

Talk about It

▶ How is today's Bible verse a lot like yesterday's verse? *(Both verses warn us to choose our friends wisely because their behavior can rub off on us.)*

▶ How can friends help each other when it comes to the sin of anger? *(A good friend will help his friend by kindly pointing out an angry comment or attitude so that it doesn't become a pattern.)*

▶ Do you have a problem with anger? If so, what should you do about it? *(Parents, if your children have a tendency toward anger, help them see that every time they get mad they can ask Jesus to help them turn away from anger and they can also ask for forgiveness.)*

Pray about It

Ask God to make you wise in your choice of friends.

**Sing together
"A Good Friend."**

Verse 1
A friend will always think of others
A friend will overlook a wrong
A friend sticks closer than a brother
A friend is patient all along
Jesus, help me be the friend You are to me

Chorus
A good friend, true friend
Here to help you through friend
Strong friend, kind friend
You can have what's mine, friend
Best friend, sure friend
Humble and a pure friend
Lord, I wanna be a good friend

Verse 2
A friend will help me do the right things
A friend won't lead me into sin
A friend will help me when I stumble
A friend will lift me up again
Jesus, help me find a friend who'll make me wise

Day 3

Dig into the Word
Read Proverbs 14:20:

> *The poor are despised even by their neighbors, while the rich have many "friends." (NLT)*

Read Provers 19:4:

> *Wealth makes many "friends"; poverty drives them all away. (NLT)*

True friends are glad to serve and sacrifice for each other. But some people see a friend as someone who should give them something. They don't make friends to give to others; they make friends to get from others. Perhaps they know a friend with a brand-new dollhouse and want to go over to her house to play with it. Or they befriend someone whose parents have a pool, for swimming privileges.

In Proverbs we learn that money gets you a lot of friends who are only your friend because of what you can give them. Then, when your money is gone, those who aren't really true friends leave you.

Think about why you have the friends you do. Are you a friend of someone because of what you give to them? Or, are you a friend of someone because of what you want to get from them? Remember that only when you know Jesus and his love, can you really give yourself to others.

Jesus is the ultimate true friend. He didn't come to earth to get; he came to earth to give. Jesus gave his life for us, and he offers to be a friend to any sinner who turns away from their sin to place their trust in him (John 15:13–15).

Talk about It

▶ Why do people want to be friends with those who are rich by the world's standards? *(People are basically selfish and like to be friends with those who can give them things.)*

▶ What do you need to be a true friend? *(You need to know Jesus and his love.)*

▶ Why is Jesus a great example of a true friend? *(Jesus came to earth to give, not to get. He demonstrated his friendship by giving up his life for us.)*

Pray about It

Ask God to help you be a good friend—one who loves the Lord and enters into friendship to serve others, not for what you can get out of it for yourself.

 Day 4

Dig into the Word

Read Proverbs 20:6:

> *Many claim to have unfailing love, but a faithful person who can find? (NIV)*

When people talk about unfailing love and faithfulness in a lasting friendship, they are often talking about marriage. Learning to be a good, faithful friend when you are young will prepare you to be a good, faithful friend to your spouse, if you get married one day. It is, of course, just as important to look for these qualities in a husband or wife.

Your marriage partner should be someone with whom you can share your heart and life. You should be walking the same road in the same direction, spiritually. You should agree who rules your life together. If Jesus is *your* Savior and Lord, then your life partner should also claim Jesus as his or her Savior and Lord.

When people grow up and like someone very much and then think about marrying them, it is easy to have warm feelings for them. This is often called "falling in love." When people are "in love" it is hard to imagine that they will ever feel differently about each other. But after marriage, as life gets busy and hard and, often, boring, those early warm feelings cool. Then you must remember that even if you get mad at each other, God wants you to be a faithful friend. When you know Jesus as your faithful friend, you can be sure that he will help you be a faithful friend too.

Talk about It

▶ Why is it important to be a good, faithful friend while you're young? *(Being a good, faithful friend will prepare you for your grown-up relationships.)*

▶ Why is it important to choose a future husband or wife who pursues and desires to be faithful? *(Marriage is a friendship that we keep for life and requires us to faithfully love all our life.)*

▶ Why do you think God tells his children not to marry people who do not believe in Jesus? *(Think through some of the challenges couples have when they don't both trust Jesus.)*

Pray about It

Take time to pray for that God will teach you how to be a faithful friend right now.

Day 5

Dig into the Word

Read John 15:12–15:

> *This is my commandment, that you love one another as I have loved you. Greater love has no one than this, that someone lay down his life for his friends. You are my friends if you do what I command you. No longer do I call you servants, for the servant does not know what his master is doing; but I have called you friends, for all that I have heard from my Father I have made known to you.*

Just before his crucifixion, Jesus spoke to his disciples, calling them his friends. Jesus said that friendship is about giving to the other person. Of course Jesus was pointing to his own death on the cross. He wanted to let his disciples, and all of us, know that his death was an act of love for us. Jesus died on the cross as the ultimate act of loving friendship. Jesus wants to be our best friend. For his part, he gave up his life for us. For our part, we must trust him, turn away from our sin, and follow him.

Just as Jesus laid down his life for us, he wants us to lay down our lives for him. Jesus said: "If anyone wishes to come after Me, he must deny himself, and take up his cross daily and follow Me" (Luke 9:23 NASB).

This doesn't mean we are all going to die on a cross. It does mean, however, that we all must die to whatever we are tempted to love more than Jesus. Jesus doesn't just want to be a friend; Jesus wants to be our *best* friend.

Talk about It

▶ Who is your best friend?

▶ What did Jesus do to show us his friendship? *(Jesus laid down his life for us; he died on the cross for our sins.)*

▶ How do we become a friend of Jesus? *(Parents, help your children understand that we need to do two things to become a friend of Jesus. First, we must turn away from sin. Second, we must believe and put our trust in Jesus. After all, how can you be a friend of someone you neither believe nor trust?)*

▶ Parents, when did you first consider Jesus to be your friend? *(Share your spiritual journey with your children. Many people grow up afraid of God, thinking only of him as a judge. But once the Spirit of God comes to live inside of us, we think of Jesus as our friend.)*

Pray about It

Ask God to help you understand what it means to have Jesus as your best friend.

Week 11

Honesty Is the Best Policy

Learning to Speak the Truth

Day 1

Dig into the Word
Read Proverbs 6:16–19:

> *There are six things that the LORD hates, seven that are*
> *an abomination to him: haughty eyes, a lying tongue,*
> *and hands that shed innocent blood, a heart that devises*
> *wicked plans, feet that make haste to run to evil, a false*
> *witness who breathes out lies, and one who sows discord*
> *among brothers.*

Here is a list of things that God is against. Notice that lying appears not once but twice on the list (a "lying tongue" and a "false witness who pours out lies"). This list helps us to understand what God wants his people to look like. As God's people we should love what God loves, and hate what God hates. But how can we do this? It's impossible to think the way God does, isn't it?

The answer is that God has given us his Holy Spirit. Romans 8:5 says, "Those who are dominated by the sinful nature think about sinful things, but those who are controlled by the Holy Spirit think about things that please the Spirit" (NLT). The Holy Spirit teaches us how to love what God loves and hate what God hates. He teaches us how to be holy.

Now, back to lying. The truth is that we all stumble and tell lies sometimes—big lies, little lies, and in-between lies. Does today's passage mean that when we lie—when we sin—God automatically hates us? No! If you belong to God—if you are his child—he will always love you. You cannot do anything to make God love you more or love you less. But, if you lie, lie, and lie some more and think that is fine, maybe you don't belong to God after all. Because when you belong to God and have the Holy Spirit inside, he teaches you to be against the things that God is against.

As God's child, when we tell lies we need to confess our sin to him and ask for forgiveness. God's grace is inexhaustible—that means it never runs out. Not only do we need to ask for forgiveness, but we need to ask for help to love what God loves and hate what God hates.

Talk about It

▶ What is lying? *(Lying is when you don't tell the truth.)*

▶ Why do you think lying is a sin? *(God is all about truth. His word is truth, he is Truth and God cannot lie.)*

▶ What should a child of God do when she lies? *(The child of God must go to him for forgiveness and help, trusting that Jesus took the penalty for that sin when he died on the cross, just as he took the penalty for every other sin.)*

Pray about It

Ask God to help you recognize and confess your sin and trust him to teach you how to love what he loves and hate what he hates.

True or False

Supplies: piece of straight wire (a large, brand-new twisty tie works fine)

The purpose of this object lesson is to show how easy it is to bend a wire, so it is no longer "true" or straight. It is nearly impossible to make it perfectly straight again once it has been bent. Likewise it is easy to tell a lie and lose someone's trust, and much harder to regain a person's trust afterward.

Ask your children what the word *true* means. Then explain how it can be used to describe something that is perfectly straight. For instance, carpenters look down the end of a board to see if the board is true or straight. Looking down a long board makes it easier to see if the board twists or bows.

Tell your children that it is easy to trust a person who always tells the truth. But, once a person lies, then you never know if they are lying or telling the truth. Regaining trust takes a lot of time. It is easy to tell a lie, but much harder to straighten out your reputation.

Pass around the straight wire and have everyone look down the end to see if it is true. Ask, "How hard do you think it is to bend the wire. How hard is it to make it true again?

Allow the children to put two or three bends in the wire. Then have

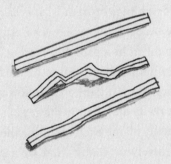

them try and make the wire true. They will see just how hard it is.

Explain that this week's lesson is about what God tells us about telling the truth in his Word.

Day 2

Dig into the Word
Read Proverbs 12:17–19:

> *An honest witness tells the truth; a false witness tells lies. Some people make cutting remarks, but the words of the wise bring healing. Truthful words stand the test of time, but lies are soon exposed. (NLT)*

Did you ever get caught having an argument or fight with one of your siblings or friends? It is easy to get angry and say things that are unkind. Did you ever notice, when you were caught in the argument by a parent or teacher, how difficult it is to tell the truth? Our natural instinct is to blame it on the other person and tell the story of what happened in a way that makes us look better than we really are. That is the reason people involved in an argument usually blame each other for the conflict and rarely accept blame themselves. Really what we are doing is lying and giving false testimony.

We all get caught in sin from time to time. But how we respond when we are caught in our sin says a lot about who we trust. Those who lie are more concerned about themselves than others they've hurt or God. But when you admit your fault and tell the truth, you bless those you've wronged and honor God.

When people think of false testimony, they usually think of an official trial when a lawyer asks a witness to tell what he or she saw, and instead of telling the truth the witness tells a lie. But you don't need a courtroom to give false testimony. Anytime your mom or dad asks what happened or what's going on, and you don't tell the truth, you are giving false testimony. Remember from yesterday, "God hates a false witness who pours out lies."

**Sing together
"To Tell the Truth."**

Chorus
To tell the truth is what I want to do
Because You love the lips that speak the truth
To tell a lie leads me away from You
So help me, God, to tell the truth

Verse 1
Your Words will last forever
They never change or fade
You never break a promise
We can trust all You say
But when my words aren't truthful
I'm doing something wrong
They'll only last a moment
Suddenly they'll be gone

Verse 2
A little lie seems harmless
Like ordinary words
But lies we tell to others
Are like a sword that hurts
When someone tries to tell me
That covering up's okay
Don't let me be dishonest
Help me to humbly say

Music and words by Bob Kauflin and Stephen Altrogge. © 2010 Sovereign Grace Praise (BMI). Sovereign Grace Music, a division of Sovereign Grace Churches. All rights reserved. Administrated worldwide at www. CapitolCMGPublishing.com, excluding the UK which is adm. by Integrity Music, part of the David C Cook family. www.SovereignGraceMusic.org

(From *Walking with the Wise*, http://www.sovereigngracemusic.org/Albums/Walking_with_the_Wise?pp=1|2)

Solomon compared our lies against one another to stabbing each other with a sword. It hurts when someone lies about you and gets you in trouble. You can't always make everything right, but you can always own up to your part in a conflict and tell the truth. Doing so can bring healing between you and the person you were in the conflict with. But even if it doesn't, you can always pray for the person who hurt you. That's what Jesus calls loving your enemies.

Talk about It

▶ Recall a time when you got caught in a conflict or fight and were tempted to lie to make it look like it was the other person's fault. *(Parents, draw out your children here. Help them remember a conflict where they blamed their friend or sibling instead of first telling what they did wrong.)*

▶ Why do we lie about our part in a fight or conflict? *(We are trying to protect ourselves. In that moment we are the most important person—following God and his truth becomes less important.)*

▶ What should we do when caught in a fight or conflict and someone asks, "What happened?" *(We should always tell the truth and share what we did that was wrong, rather than pointing out what the other person did wrong. It is important not to exaggerate the other person's guilt.)*

Pray about It

Ask God to help you be a truthful witness and tell the truth when you are caught in a conflict.

Day 3

Dig into the Word

Read Proverbs 12:20–22:

> *Deceit is in the heart of those who devise evil, but those who plan peace have joy. No ill befalls the righteous, but the wicked are filled with trouble. Lying lips are an abomination to the* Lord, *but those who act faithfully are his delight.*

Proverbs tells us that lying, or deceit, doesn't come from what's happening outside us; it comes from what's inside us. Jesus also taught that lying flows from our hearts: "But the things that come out of a person's mouth come from the heart. Those are the things that make someone 'unclean.' Evil thoughts come out of a person's heart. So do murder, adultery, and other sexual sins. And so do stealing, bearing false witness, and telling lies about others" (Matthew 15:18–19 NIrV).

Every lie we speak flows out of the sin in our hearts. Unless we confess our lies, we will often have to keep lying to keep from getting caught. One lie is not usually enough. We have to keep up making stories to try and prove that our original story is true. We do this because instead of wanting God, we want the things of the world. We use lying to try and get what we want, or to protect us when we are caught in our sin.

Whenever you get caught doing something wrong you are faced with a choice: will you tell the truth about what you've done, or will you lie to escape consequences or maybe just to make yourself look better? Whichever you decide tells what is in your heart.

As sinners, our hearts are desperately wicked. That is why we need the Holy Spirit to change our hearts. We all need the Holy

Spirit to keep watch over our hearts and help us tell the truth out of love for Jesus.

Talk about It

▶ Where do lies come from? *(Lies flow out of our sinful hearts.)*

▶ How does the Holy Spirit help us? *(The Holy Spirit is working at changing our hearts so that we don't want to sin and so that we repent quickly when we do.)*

▶ How can we receive the Holy Spirit? *(God promises to give his Spirit to anyone who believes that Jesus died for their sin.)*

Pray about It

Ask God to help you turn away from your sin and believe in Jesus.

 Day 4

Dig into the Word

Read Proverbs 8:6–8:

> *Listen to me! For I have important things to tell you. Everything I say is right, for I speak the truth and detest every kind of deception. My advice is wholesome. There is nothing devious or crooked in it. (NLT)*

Did you ever hear the saying "Do what I say, not what I do"? Or, "Practice what you preach"? The writer of the scripture verses we are looking at today insists that he speaks the truth. It is easy, however, to speak the truth; it is much harder to *live* the truth.

Take Solomon, for example. Solomon wrote many wise sayings. He wrote, "The wages of the righteous is life, but the earnings of the wicked are sin and death (Proverbs 10:16). Even though King Solomon wrote these wise, truthful words, he hired craftsman to build idols for his foreign wives to worship. So Solomon taught one thing and did another. That is living a lie.

This is the same for us as well. It is easy to speak wise, righteous words; it is much harder (impossible, in fact) to live a wise, righteous life. This is why we need Jesus who is "the way, the truth, and the life." Jesus lived the wise, righteous life we could never live. On the cross Jesus took the punishment that we (and that King Solomon) deserved for our sin. Trusting in Jesus is the only way to be made righteous in God's eyes. God gives us the Holy Spirit. It is the Holy Spirit who grows godly fruit in our hearts and lives.

Talk about It

▶ What do you think is easier, speaking the truth or living the truth? *(Words are easy to say, but it is more difficult to live a truthful life. What we say shows what is in our head; how we live shows what lies deep in our heart.)*

▶ Read together Galatians 5:22–23. What kind of fruit does the Holy Spirit grow in the hearts of God's children? *(The Holy Spirit produces love, joy, peace, patience, kindness, goodness, faithfulness, gentleness, and self-control.)*

▶ Share a time when you said one thing, but then did something else. *(Parents, share your own struggles. Then help your children think through how they have similar struggles.)*

Pray about It

Ask God to help you both speak the truth, and live the truth you speak.

Day 5

Dig into the Word
Read John 14:6:

> *I am the way, and the truth, and the life. No one comes to the Father except through me.*

The night before he was crucified, Jesus told his disciples that he was leaving to go back to his Father in heaven. Thomas was confused and said he didn't understand where Jesus was going or how to get there. Jesus said that he was the Way, and the Truth, and the Life.

The world claims that there are many ways to God. But that's a lie. Jesus is the only Way. And, just in case we are tempted to doubt Jesus, he calls himself the Truth. Jesus spoke the truth, lived the truth, and taught the truth about how we can be saved.

Jesus never lied; he obeyed God perfectly in everything. Jesus always kept his word and lived out the teaching he called others to follow. For example, Jesus told people to love their enemies and pray for those who persecuted them (Matthew 5:44). And Jesus did exactly that. He died on the cross for his enemies (Romans 5:8). While hanging on the cross, Jesus prayed for those who were killing him when he said, "Father forgive them, for they know not what they do" (Luke 23:34).

Jesus died on the cross to take the punishment we deserve for our sin against God. Jesus lived a perfect life and offers to exchange his righteousness for the sin of anyone who repents and trusts in him. Trusting in Jesus is the only way to God.

Lies are about trying to earn your own salvation. We tell lies to get out of trouble and hide sin, but speaking the truth about our sin is necessary before we can go to Jesus. We tell lies to get things we want, but only Jesus the Truth brings lasting joy. If we tell lies to build ourselves up, we are trying to find some other way to God.

Boasting in Jesus is the only way to eternal life. When we tell the truth, we are standing with Jesus, who *is* the Truth.

Talk about It

▶ How did Jesus both speak the truth and live the truth? *(He always practiced what he preached. For example, he told others to love their enemies, and then himself showed love for his enemies.)*

▶ What did Jesus mean when he said "I am the truth"? *(Jesus spoke the truth, lived the truth, and taught the truth about how we can be saved. He was saying that he was God and that his very essence is truth.)*

▶ Why do we need Jesus? *(Parents, help your children to see that we all tell lies and our only hope is to turn away from our sins and turn to Jesus.)*

Pray about It

Ask God to help you live your life for Jesus, who is the truth, the life, and the only way to the Father in heaven.

Week 12

God Is Love

Loving as God Loves

Day 1

Dig into the Word
Read Proverbs 10:12:

Hatred stirs up conflict, but love covers over all wrongs.
(NIV)

What if a small child got hold of a permanent black marker and scribbled all over one of the walls in your house? What would you do? You can't clean permanent marker off the walls. There is only one solution: cover up the black marks with paint.

Today's proverb tells us that if you love someone, you will cover up the wrongs they do. Just like paint covers the black marks, when we forgive someone for hurting us, we cover over their sin and choose to live as though it never happened.

Showing anger or hatred toward a person for sinning against us leads to conflict, which is kind of like a fight. Think of a baseball pitcher who hits a batter with the ball. If the batter charges the pitcher in anger, it usually leads to all kinds of problems. The rest of the players might jump onto the field to fight, and the batter could be thrown out of the game. But if he covers the offense of the pitcher for hitting him and just walks to first base, the game can continue without a problem.

In the same way, God wants us to really love others by covering the wrongs they've done to us. Remember, God covered over our sins. He wants us to treat others the way we ourselves have been treated.

Talk about It

▶ What does it mean to cover someone's sin against you? *(We choose to forgive a person's sin when we cover it, just as a fresh coat of paint covers the scribble of a toddler on the wall.)*

▶ Can you think of a time when someone covered your sin? *(Parents, try to help your children think of a time when they broke something or got angry and you or a brother or sister forgave them instead of getting angry.)*

▶ What can happen when we refuse to forgive? *(Refusing to forgive only leads to more conflict and fights.)*

Pray about It

Ask God to help you cover over the sins of people who offend you.

 Day 2

....

Dig into the Word

Read Proverbs 17:9:

> *Whoever wants to show love forgives a wrong. But those who talk about it separate close friends. (NIrV)*

Today's verse reminds us that our goal as children of God is to love God and love others. God has called us as his people to live for him in such a way that the world looks at us and sees Jesus. One of the ways we can show Jesus to the world is to practice forgiveness. God has forgiven our sins for Jesus's sake, and we are called to forgive others.

Scrubbed Clean

Supplies: melamine foam cleaning sponge (e.g., Magic Eraser), water in a bucket, paper towels

Look for the grimiest wall, door, or doorjamb in your house or garage. Then call your children to do a little cleaning experiment. Explain to your children that the day-to-day grime of their hands over time dirties the wall (or door). It happens so slowly that we often don't realize how dirty the wall becomes until it gets really dirty.

Explain to the children that the wall is a lot like our sin. Unless God touches our heart and forgives our sin, our sin grows and grows. But when we put our faith in Jesus and confess our sin, he promises to forgive us and to cleanse us of our sin (1 John 1:9).

Demonstrate how the sponge works by scrubbing an area of the wall in the shape of their first initial. Wipe it clean and see if you can read the clean letter against the dirty background.

When you use the cleaning sponge on the wall, the sponge is worn away. So, in order to take the dirt away, you have to sacrifice or give up the sponge. (The cleaning sponge is made of a plastic called melamine that has been made into foam. When melamine is formed into foam, it has microscopic, sharp edges that wear away as it scrapes the dirt off.) As you clean, the sponge is worn away.

This is a little picture of how we are saved through Jesus's sacrifice. We can be cleansed of our sin because he was willing to sacrifice himself for us.

The Bible tells us that when God forgives us, he "remembers our sins no more" (Hebrews 8:12). He removes them "as far from us as the east is from the west" (Psalm 103:12 NLT). When we forgive someone, we agree not to bring the offense up again in an angry, bitter way. We agree not to hold what they did against them, or talk about it with others in a mean way.

Forgiveness is something we need to practice every day. If we don't forgive someone and cover their offense, then we are likely to do just the opposite—gossip about it to others. But gossiping about someone's sin against us can destroy a friendship. Forgiveness builds a friendship. An unforgiving spirit is a place where bitterness, gossip, and evil can grow unchecked.

Do you think you have forgiven someone who has wronged you? Having angry thoughts about them or gossiping about them are signals that you need to forgive them again. Often forgiveness is something that we have to do over and over.

Talk about It

▶ What are some warning signs that we have not really forgiven someone? *(Angry, bitter thoughts, and gossip are some signs that we have not really forgiven someone for a wrong against us.)*

▶ Why is it so important to forgive others? *(Forgiving others shows us how well we understand how much God has forgiven us.)*

▶ When God forgave you, did he have a lot to forgive or only a little bit? *(When we sin, what we are really saying is that we can do a better job at being God than God can. There's no such thing as a little sin.)*

Pray about It

Ask God to help you understand more about how much you have been forgiven. Ask him to teach you how to forgive others.

Day 3

Dig into the Word

Read Proverbs 15:1–4:

> *A gentle answer turns away wrath, But a harsh word stirs up anger. The tongue of the wise makes knowledge acceptable, But the mouth of fools spouts folly. The eyes of the LORD are in every place, Watching the evil and the good. A soothing tongue is a tree of life, But perversion in it crushes the spirit. (NASB)*

Imagine sitting in the car next to your brother. What do you do if your brother starts swinging his leg and kicks you? You are already uncomfortable in such a tight space and his careless actions annoy you. If you say something mean, you are likely going to start a fight, and the rest of the trip could turn into one big conflict. But if you speak gently, and ask him to please stop swinging his leg, he is much more likely to listen.

What if you were the one swinging your leg in that same tight space and hit your brother, and he exploded in anger at you? If you respond with a harsh word, you are in for a fight. But if you apologize with a gentle answer, he is likely to calm down.

It is in our very nature to be quick to get angry and slow to forgive. This is the very opposite of what God is like. God is "slow to anger and filled with unfailing love . . . He does not deal harshly with us as we deserve" (Psalm 103:8, 10 NLT). Keep in mind that others can hurt us like we have hurt God. When we understand how much God loves us and how much he has forgiven us, then we are able to forgive others who have hurt us.

Sing together
"Who Can Say."

Verse 1
Who can say, "I have made my heart pure
I am clean from my sin"?
No one's blameless in God's holy eyes
That's why the Savior came

Chorus
Jesus, Jesus, only You did everything right
Jesus, Jesus, died and rose
So we could have new life

Verse 2
Who has perfectly followed God's law
Loving all of His ways?
The One who gave up His life in our place
Jesus, the King who saves

WHO
CAN
SAY

From *Walking with the Wise*, http://www.

sp
you
apo
It
forgive
get ang
with us,
no one ca
how much
we will be a

Talk about It

▶ Can you remember a time when someone did something against you that made you angry and you responded harshly? *(Parents, children do this all the time, especially when you restrict their behavior. Help them think back to a time when they got angry and said something disrespectful or harsh to you or a sibling.)*

▶ How does God respond to us when we sin against him? *(God is slow to anger and filled with love. He forgives us when we confess and turn away from sin.)*

▶ How should we respond when someone sins against us? *(We should be slow to anger and speak gentle words.)*

Pray about It

Ask God to help you understand how much you have been forgiven.

 Day 4

Dig into the Word

Read 1 John 4:9–11:

> *This is how God showed his love among us: He sent his one and only Son into the world that we might live through him. This is love: not that we loved God, but that he loved us and sent his Son as an atoning sacrifice for our sins. Dear friends, since God so loved us, we also ought to love one another. (NIV)*

Because of his amazing love for us, God sent his Son Jesus to die for our sins so we could be forgiven. Remember John 3:16? "For God so loved the world, that he gave his only Son, that whoever believes in him should not perish but have eternal life." God sent his Son and offers forgiveness of sins through Jesus's death because of his great love for us.

Not only did God send his Son for our forgiveness, now God tells us to love one another in the same way. In so many words John is saying, "Because God sent his Son to die on the cross to cover your sins, you should show the same love to others by covering their sins."

It is easy to say, "I forgive you." It is much harder to actually forgive someone in our heart. Forgiving is more than saying words. Sure, the words are important, but if we hold bitterness and anger in our heart against a person for what they did to us, we are not really forgiving them.

The best way to forgive a person who has sinned against us is to remember how much we ourselves have been forgiven by God. No matter how many times we sin against God, he never refuses to forgive us. We forgive others because God has forgiven us. Sometimes we hold back forgiveness because someone has not asked for forgiveness or because we don't think someone's apology is good enough or because we don't think the person deserves our forgiveness. We might even say we forgive them, but then hold back loving them. We need to remember that forgiveness is a free gift that we do not earn. God extended forgiveness to us out of love, and we should extend forgiveness to others out of love.

The apostle Paul tells us in 1 Corinthians 13 that love is the most important quality we can demonstrate with our lives. We might be the smartest, or wisest, or most gifted person in the whole world, but if we don't show love toward others, we are like an annoying, crashing cymbal. Simply put, showing love toward one another is the greatest thing we can do.

Talk about It

▶ How has God shown his love to us? (*God sent Jesus to die for us so that our sins could be washed away and we could be his children.*)

▶ Is it ever OK not to forgive someone? (*God has forgiven us freely, and he wants us to forgive others freely also.)*

▶ How can we know that we have really forgiven someone? *(We will not think about them with bitterness and anger; we will not gossip about them; we will look for ways to show love to them.)*

▶ What are some ways we can demonstrate love to one another? *(Parents, draw your children out on this one. You can read them 1 Corinthians 13 to help them broaden their answer.)*

Pray about It
Thank God for sending his only Son Jesus to die in our place so we can be forgiven.

 Day 5

Dig into the Word
Read 1 Peter 4:7–11:

> *Be watchful and control yourselves. Then you may pray. Most of all, love one another deeply. Love erases many sins by forgiving them. Welcome others into your homes without complaining. God's gifts of grace come in many forms. Each of you has received a gift in order to serve others. You should use it faithfully. If anyone speaks, they should do it as one speaking God's words. If anyone serves, they should do it with the strength God provides. Then in all things God will be praised through Jesus Christ. Glory and power belong to him for ever and ever. (NIrV)*

The apostle Peter reminds us, "love erases many sins by forgiving them." When we forgive we glorify Christ because forgiving is loving others as God has loved us (1 John 4:11).

When Peter asked Jesus how many times we should forgive someone who sins against us, Jesus replied, "Seventy-seven times" (Matthew 18:22). Jesus didn't mean we should keep count of how many times we forgive a person and stop forgiving them at number 77. Jesus picked a large number to help us see we need to keep forgiving no matter how many times we are sinned against. For those of us who have turned away from our sin to trust in Jesus, God forgives all of our sins, even though we have sinned against God way more than 77 times.

When Proverbs says "love covers over all wrongs" (Proverbs 10:12 NIV), it looks forward to the day that God's love would cover our sins. All forgiveness finds its beginning in the forgiveness God brought to us. We love because God first loved us (1 John 4:19).

Talk about It

▶ How did God demonstrate his love for us? *(God sent Jesus to die on the cross so that we can be forgiven.)*

▶ How can we show we know God has forgiven us? *(When we forgive others we are showing that we know we ourselves have been forgiven by God.)*

▶ What does it feel like when someone forgives you for something bad that you have done? *(Parents, draw out your children here. They can either remember a real-life situation or imagine what it would be like to do something sinful toward someone and then be forgiven.)*

Pray about It

Thank God for sending his Son Jesus to die on the cross and take our punishment so that we can be forgiven.